CW01073143

in full
COLOUR

Recent Buildings and Interiors

Imprint
The Deutsche Bibliothek is registering this publication in the
Deutsche Nationalbibliographie; detailed bibliographical infor-
mation can be found on the internet at http://dnb.ddb.de

ISBN 978-3-938780-33-6

© 2008 by Verlagshaus Braun
www.verlagshaus-braun.de

The work is copyright protected. Any use outside of the close
boundaries of the copyright law, which has not been granted
permission by the publisher, is unauthorized and liable for pros-
ecution. This especially applies to duplications, translations, mi-
crofilming, and any saving or processing in electronic systems.

1st edition 2008

Editorial staff:
Anna Hinc, Jacob Hochrein, Susanne Laßwitz, Sophie Steybe
Translation:
Stephen Roche, Hamburg
Graphic concept and layout:
Michaela Prinz
Reproduction:
LVD Gesellschaft für Datenverarbeitung mbH, Berlin

All of the information in this volume has been compiled to
the best of the editors knowledge. It is based on the information provided to the publisher by the architects' and designers' offices and excludes any liability. The publisher assumes
no responsibility for its accuracy or completeness as well as
copyright discrepancies and refers to the specified sources
(architects and designers offices). All rights to the photographs
are property of the photographer (please refer to the picture
credit).

in full COLOUR

Recent Buildings and Interiors

Projects selected by
Dirk Meyhöfer

BRAUN

"There is nothing that inspires the colours. I know of no relationship between function and colour for example, except for blackness of death. A good session using paint will end with a suggestion of a possibility for an architectural project. This does not mean necessarily an image. I am trying to get excited about a response to an opportunity that goes beyond style and beyond known architecture. In this sense the use of paint is very similar to working in workshops with the general public."

Will Alsop, architect and painter, London

Colour is relative, colour is emotional…

Colour in architecture, architecture and colour – this is a vast field, occasionally even a love-hate relationship; but always a fascinating area of activity for architects and designers. After all, colour by its very nature – whether its effect is cool or warm, light or dark, introverted or extroverted – is defined through the interplay of light and shade, through location and other environmental influences. In other words, colour changes with its surroundings. Red, for example, is never the same tone, but changes depending on the surface material and the neighbouring surfaces that may swallow or reflect light. Many modern architects have an ambivalent attitude to colour. The more dogmatic among them, according to the Düsseldorf architect Niklaus Fritschi, "risk losing sight of the essential behind an attitude of black, white and grey abstinence, risk losing the audience because of hollow 'asceticism'". It is a known fact that architecture has a history of disregarding colour.

For many years art historians were convinced that architecture in the Classical World was without colour. As a result, they laid down a line of defined form and colourless fidelity to material that held sway right up to the period of Classical Modernism.

It has since been proven that neither in the Ancient World nor in Gothic or Renaissance architecture was colour ever quite abandoned. As early as 1830 the architect Jacques Ignace Hittorff described the use of colour in Greek buildings in his work, "De l'Architecture Polychrome chez les Grecs". His thesis was supported by archaeological finds at Pompeii, Paestum, Selinunt and other ancient sites, where colourful fragments of buildings and figures were discovered. All architecture,

from prehistoric times to the end of the Baroque era, involved some use of colour. The ubiquity of colour among ancient cultures is manifested in the temples, statues and reliefs of the Egyptians, as well as in the surviving works of the Sumerian, Babylonian, Assyrian and Persian civilisations.

Western civilisation and what is arguably its most significant architectural form, the Gothic cathedral, was largely seen and experienced in a colourless and sanitised state in the nineteenth century. This view produced a distorted image, likewise of ecclesiastical Romanesque architecture. The secular buildings of the German Renaissance were at one time elaborately adorned in colour, which was used on individual decorative elements (pilasters, plinths, etc.) to clearly set them apart from the walls. The colourfulness of Baroque architecture is beyond dispute, as it is well preserved in numerous specimens. It is a general rule that a purist era will be succeeded by a colourful one. The Classical Modern period of the twentieth century took over from the excessive, kitsch eclecticism of the nineteenth century and sought new meaning in abstraction and reduction. But the ideology of prevention leads down a cul-de-sac. That luminary of twentieth century architecture, Le Corbusier, predicted in 1928 that colour would eventually attain equal status with form as a design medium. This, he believed, would result in the creation of continuous spaces. Colour, he maintained, helped to expand and modify spaces, to articulate their volume, and ultimately entered into a dialectic relationship with space.

Today, following the end of the early modern period and the hedonism of the 1980s, it is no longer possible

6

to imagine architecture without colour. It is now used in a precise and controlled manner in both interior and exterior architecture. This is clearly demonstrated by the selection of coloured buildings and colour-inspired projects from the last five years that are included in this book.

Our kaleidoscope of coloured (rather than colourful) buildings spans the entire world – both the northern and southern hemispheres – and therefore includes a corresponding range of natural lighting conditions. It includes the opulent colour tones that have particularly dominated Mexican architecture since Luis Barragán. It includes European rationalism which recognised that colour has an organisational function, that it can help to provide orientation within a building, and even help to repair or mitigate architectural errors made in the original building. It is therefore no surprise that this collection includes numerous school buildings, where colour is often required to radiate more cheer than the otherwise grey surroundings are capable of. In a similar way, the Dutch star architect Ben van Berkel succeeded in overcoming the dreariness of sixties' residential developments with his blazing new red-yellow agora in Lelystad.

Form or colour – building volumes are strengthened or reduced by the application of colour. It helps, in a very emotional way, to elaborate plasticity and emphasises sculpture.

This brings us to the heart of the matter (see also Le Corbusier). Particularly through the warmth or coolness of a given colour – or rather a given colour family – or through the choice of several, interrelated colour families, a building can be endowed with a 'soul'. In architecture this is generally regarded as the ambit of space and light. Yet colour too can be a kind of catalyst, and perhaps even more. Colour focuses attention. Every observer first separates the essential from the inessential (from their own standpoint), allowing their eyes to alternately linger or wander. Here it is important to remember that colour has semantic significance; in other words, it is coded.

Red has a strongly masculine aspect, it is hot and explosive, denoting vigorous, life-giving energy. This is no milieu in which to while away peaceful hours, unless of course the red is subdued in warm brown tones. Blue is calming – the deeper the tone, the more it beckons us towards the infinite – awakening a longing for purity and transcendence. Blue is the colour of the universe, of the sky (and heavens). It is the colour we associate with the word 'heaven'. Blue, quite simply, is heavenly. Yellow, on the other hand, denotes movement and transcending boundaries. A core characteristic of the colour yellow is the dispersion of energy into our surroundings. It is also an essential earth colour.

Colour does not mean the same thing in every context; rather it is open to 'declension' in a variety of ways. Just as a word can be declined differently within a sentence depending on the grammatical context, a particular colour may convey a different meaning depending on the 'case' to which it is assigned.

In choosing a colour scheme the architect always tries to establish a particular relationship with the visitor or user – essentially suggesting coolness or warmth a priori. The choice of colour family determines whether a building appears 'cool' (reserved, functional and clearly-defined), or 'warm' (stimulating, communicative, inviting). A building's 'emotional expression' can be found in the composition of different colour tones within a single colour family or between related ones. At the same time, each person who comes in contact with the building will experience this expression differently – as indeed this book proves. I'll leave the last word to Rem Koolhaas, that pace-setter among 21st-century urban planners: "It is only logical that, with the incredible sensorial onslaught that bombards us every day and the artificial intensities that we encounter in the virtual world, the nature of colour should change, no longer just a thin layer of change, but something that genuinely alters perception. In this sense, the future of colours is looking bright."

Dirk Meyhöfer

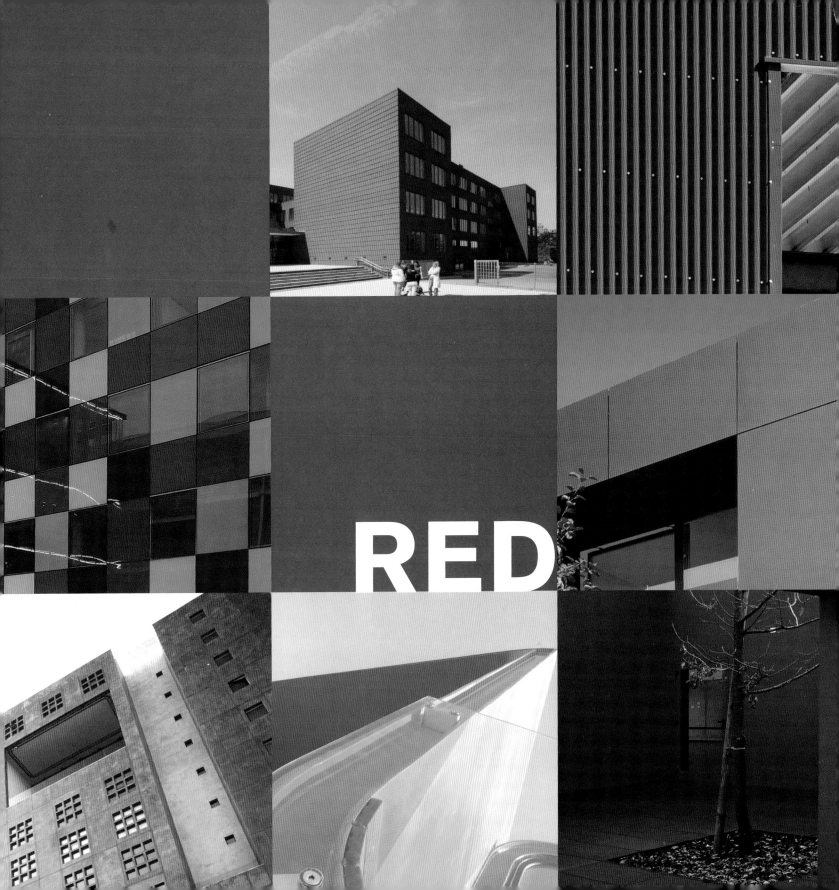

RED

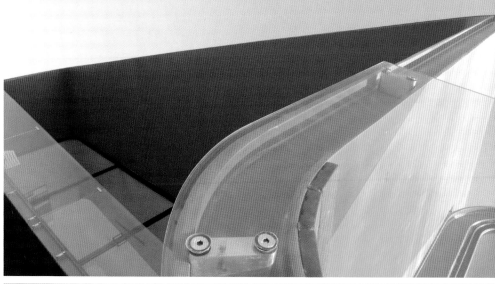

House, 2003
Residential building
Address: Tecamachalco, Estado de México, Mexico City. **Gross floor area:** 136 m². **Materials:** metal structure; cladding: rolled steel plate.

... it just had to be red!
ARCHITECTS: rojkindarquitectos, Mexico City

Located in Tecamachalco estado de México, on a hillside over looking Bosques de Reforma, an existing residential house from the 1960s was remodelled and extended. Resembling a ballet dance of two bodies in motion, the looping sensual forms that change angles coming out of every curve were inspired by the professional ballet dancer who will inhabit the house. The house is separated into two split-levels; the first containing the kitchen, dining and living areas; the second the TV room and master bedroom. In remodelling the house the architects took advantage of the roof of the existing house and its skylights. This roof is converted to a patio with the remaining chipped lava rocks used for the main wall of the house. The colour symbolises the client's passion for life ... it just had to be red. Rojkind Arquitectos use colour to accentuate emotions, in ways that vary depending on the particular clients and projects.

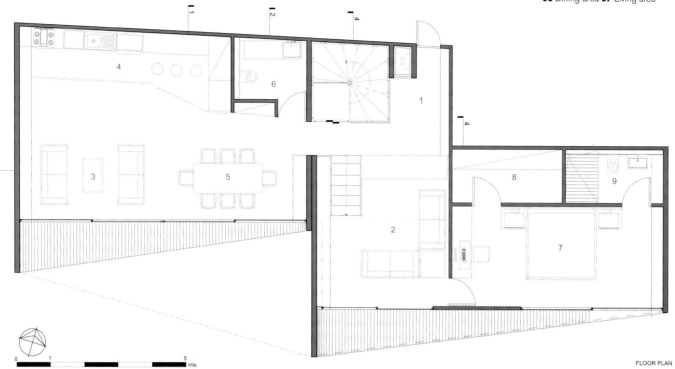

FLOOR PLAN

1.main entrance 2.t.v.room1 3.living room2 4.kitchen 5.dining room 6.guest bathroom 7.master restroom 8.dressing room 9.master bathroom

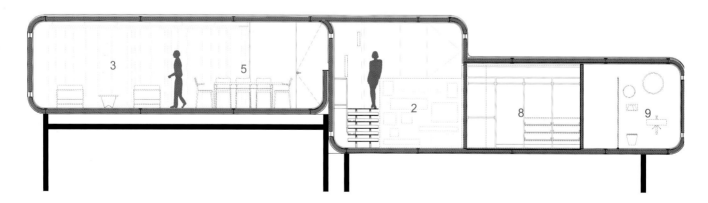

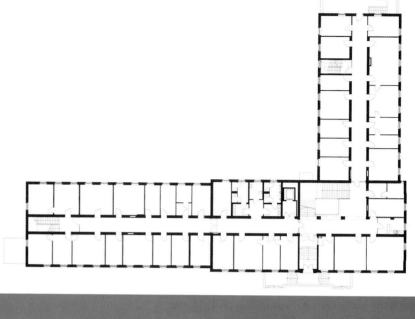

Interior Ministry of the State of Brandenburg, Potsdam, 2004
Address: Henning-von-Tresckow-Strasse 9–13, 14467 Potsdam, Germany. **Client:** Brandenburg Ministry of Finance, represented by the Public Property and Building Authority, Potsdam. **Gross floor area:** 6,000 m². **Materials:** Extension of solid structure: steel frame.

A barracks converted (turning swords to ploughshares)
ARCHITECTS: SEHW Berlin Hamburg Wien

One application of the maxim "to turn swords into ploughshares" is the conversion of military barracks to non-military use. The Interior Ministry building for the state of Brandenburg has been created on an exposed site next to the Potsdam Lustgarten (Pleasure Gardens) on the Havel river by adding to an old Prussian barracks. The third (and from an architectural, cultural and historical point of view the most valuable) building in the ensemble is the "Knobelsdorff-Haus", a late work by Georg Wenzeslaus von Knobelsdorff from the mid-eighteenth century. The structural mass of the added stair turret fortifies the front of the building in its interplay with the handsome structure at the southern end and encloses the planned access way to the Lustgarten end of the property. Thanks to the increase in volume of the 1930s structure and the "Knobelsdorff-Haus", the property as a whole has reestablished itself within the cityscape.

01 Floor plan **02** Exterior by night **03** Staircase

FLEET 3, 2004
Workshop, office, photographic studio, loft, 2004
Address: Köhlfleet-Hauptdeich 3, 21129 Hamburg,
Germany. **Structural engineers:** Abel. **Client:** Olaf
Behrens. **Gross floor area:** 1,920 m². **Materials:** rein-
forced concrete, steel, trapezoidal sheet metal.

Surprise package

ARCHITECTS: KBNK architekten
Joachim Kähne Frank Birwe
Franz-Josef Nähring Hille Krause, Hamburg

The Behrens shipyard, a family-owned business with a
long tradition in Hamburg-Finkenwerder on the banks
of the river Elbe was on the lookout for new areas of
activity. The result is the multifunctional and versatile
Red Box; it is used as an office space that is accessed
separately via an external staircase, also housing a
drawing office, a daylight photographic studio and a
penthouse. Each floor faces the water on three sides.
A major advantage of this structure is the ease with
which the rooms can be linked together for larger
events. Not to mention the fact that visitors can arrive
by boat. The striking use of the colour red is the defining
external feature of this building. The colour scheme and
use of materials in the trapezoidal sheet metal façade
fit the image of the surrounding industrial port and provide the perfect to the white-blue North German sky, the
grey of the water and the reflections in the generous
window area.

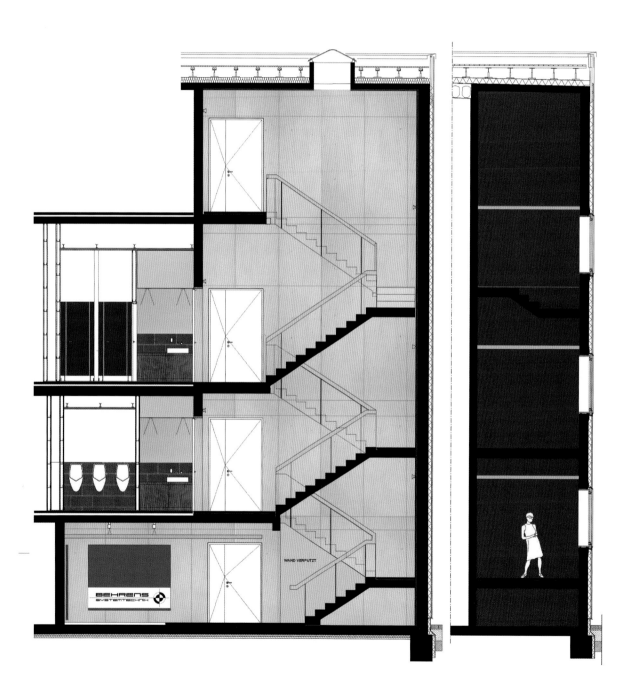

WAND VERPUTZT

BEHRENS
SYSTEMTECHNIK

Bild Box, Berlin, 2004
Address: Axel-Springer-Passage, Kochstrasse, Berlin, Germany. **Client:** Axel Springer AG, Axel-Springer-Platz 1, 20350 Hamburg. **Gross floor area:** 150 m². **Materials:** lacquered MDF; linoleum; specially designed, digitally controllable lighting.

Loud, red, rotating

ARCHITECTS: she_architekten, Hamburg

The Bild Box, a 150-square-metre fully glazed shop, acts as a showcase for Germany's largest daily newspaper beyond the protective zone of its editorial offices. The Hamburg architecture firm she_architekten wanted to produce a contrast to the existing enclosure of the Springer Passage on Kochstrasse by creating something "loud, red, rotating and ambiguous". On the basis of a complex, swinging geometry, the different functions of shop, editorial office, brand presence, Internet chat space, broadcasting studio and showcase for the BILD newspaper are arranged within a minimal floor space. All of the design elements, from the floor covering to the various built-in units and digitally controlled light fittings, combine to produce continually changing perspectives of this room in white, grey and brand-typical red that appears to rotate on a central axis.

01 Interior, congruent lines **02** Main entrance **03** Rendering, design

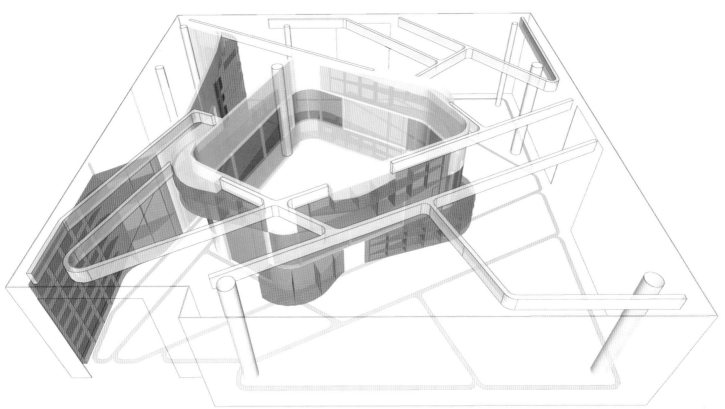

Jauch residence, 2005
Address: Sonnenblumenstrasse 20, 81377 Munich, Germany. **Gross floor area:** 277 m². **Façade:** 3 mm aluminium panels, anodised in Sandalor dark red, on strapping with 4 cm ventilation and 12 cm mineral thermal insulation.

A new coffee mill
ARCHITECTS: Gruber + Popp
Architekten BDA, Berlin

In large German cities the term "coffee mill house" is used to describe an unconventional but lovingly planned type of building built in the 1930s with a square ground plan, a tent roof, and an arris length of about 10 metres. An old building in Munich was reduced to its original structure and expanded. A view of the garden and surrounding areas, with their venerable old trees, was to be visible from deep within the new home, the heart of which is now indisputably the open kitchen. The façade of dark red anodised aluminium panels, thanks to their eloxal surfaces, provide a backdrop for the play of light, colour and shadow of the surrounding vegetation. The colour scale produced by the reflection of light on the façade ranges from an earthy reddish brown on misty autumn days to a luminous vermilion on sunny days with blue skies.

07

08

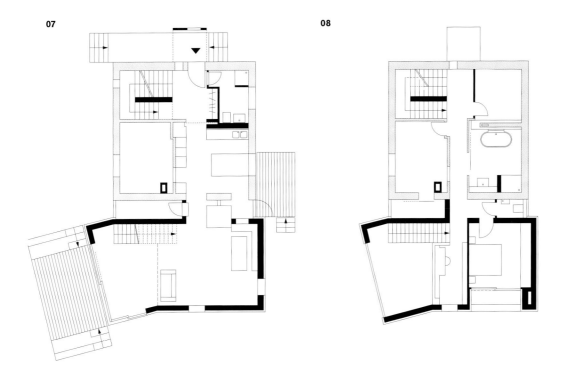

09

10

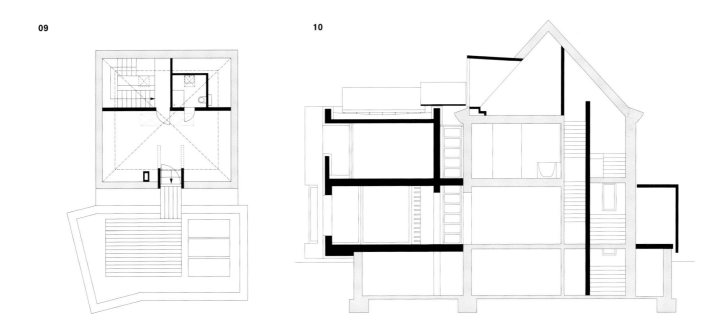

Astrid Lindgren School, Schwerin, 2003
Address: Talliner Strasse 6, 19063 Schwerin, Germany.
Client: City of Schwerin (state capital of Mecklenburg-Western Pomerania). **Gross floor area:** 5,115.8 m².
Materials: thermal insulation composite system with calcium silicate panels (rough hewn), wooden window frames, steel-glass façades.

Red as a tomato
ARCHITECTS: Roland Schulz, ars, Schwerin

The four-storey, panel constructed building housing the Astrid Lindgren School, originally completed in 1978, has been thoroughly refurbished and modernised in two stages. A roof over the existing inner and originally open-air courtyard adds the new function of an assembly hall to the old structure. The roof rests on slender columns and supports a truncated cone-shaped skylight, an improvement to the complex as a whole. The "tomato red" colour intended for the central body of the building has prevailed despite massive criticism, in the end creating a virtual exclamation mark in an otherwise drab district of prefabricated slab construction.

01 Eastern view **02** Ground floor **03** First floor **04** Eastern view **05** Schoolyard

02

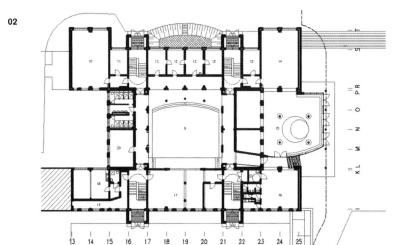

03

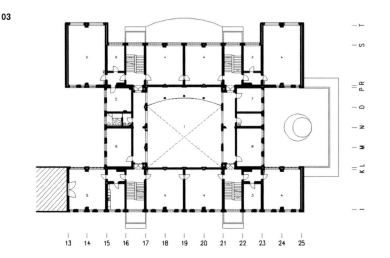

Office and commercial buildings in Falkenried, 2007
Address: Hoheluftchaussee 24, 20251 Hamburg, Germany. **Client:** STRABAG Projektentwicklung GmbH. **Materials:** reinforced concrete structure with prefabricated columns, cast-in-situ concrete girders and filigree floors built with concrete topping.

A "Wolkenbügel" for Hamburg
ARCHITECTS: Renner Hainke Wirth Architekten, Hamburg

The Yellow Office (one tenant was and remains the yellow-themed postal service) is a bold expansion of a typical specimen of "box" architecture from the 1970s in Hamburg's ambitious Falkenried district, an urban development area in amongst the popular residential districts located around Hamburg's Aussenalster, or "Outer Alster" lake. It is not yellow, however, but red. It owes its colour to its Falkenried neighbours, which consist largely of old brick factory buildings, where streetcars were once built and maintained, and new brick townhouses. This mundane, functional structure also marks the transition to a main exit road dating to the 1950s. To give it a more noble appearance, the architects have resorted to a trick: the added floors have been designed in the form of a floating "Wolkenbügel" (literally 'cloud hanger', the name originally given to a design by El Lissitzky), a kind of horizontal skyscraper. A compelling use of colour is also evident in the interior.

01 View from the Hohenluftchaussee **02** Office entrance hall **03** View of the back side

28

**Nursery school in Covolo di Pederobba,
Treviso, 2006**
Address: Covolo di Pederobba, Treviso, Italy. **Client:**
Covolo di Pederobba Municipality. **Gross floor area:**
950 m². **Materials:** yellow-grey concrete, iroko wood
and red plaster.

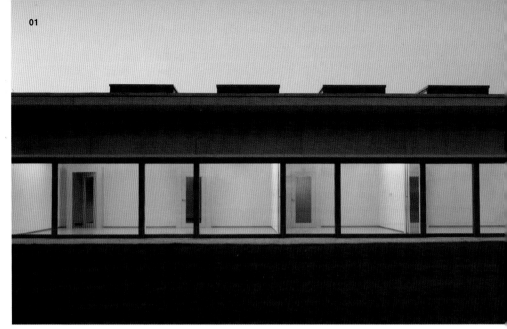

Walls and empty spaces
ARCHITECTS: C+S ASSOCIATI Architects,
Venice

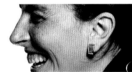

This building is its structure: a wall. A wall that retracts
and doubles, using colour to emphasize its passages, its
thresholds. Covolo landscape is a collection of modest
structures linked by a continuous series of stone walls,
held intact by a thin layer of rough plaster. These walls
run adjacent to a meandering mass of vegetation that
fills the wide gravely bed of the Piave River. Walls and
empty spaces: this is the theme of the project. Colour
outlines the door extensions and creates an orientation
grid for the children who will use the spaces. The extension of the "doors" and their colour marking introduce a
real transformation of the entrance area into an actual
space that becomes an imagined world, different and
strange, suspended between inside and out. It represents hesitation, desire, potential, wonder.

02

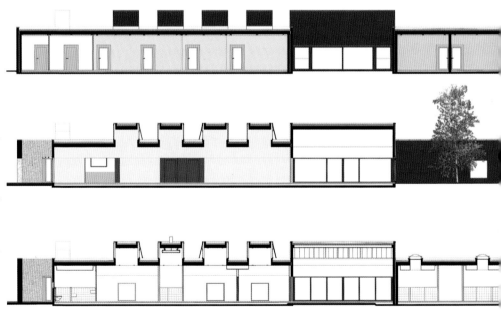

01 Detail of the south elevation **02** Sections **03** North elevation

**Faculty of Architecture, Art and Design Building,
Diego Portales University, 2004
Address:** República 180, Santiago, Chile. **Gross floor
area:** 7,283 m². **Materials:** exposed concrete and other
materials, e.g. wall curtain comprising transparent
windowpanes, both clear and coloured (black, grey,
white and red).

Dialogue with the historical structure

ARCHITECTS: Ricardo Abuauad Abujatum

This building was designed for the faculty of Architecture, Art and Design. It is located in a downtown district with strong regulations in terms of the relationship between new buildings and the architectural and historical fabric that surrounds them. Thus, the two main façades, one facing the street and the other facing the inner courtyard, respond to very different contexts. The first dialogues with the historical structures next to it, while the second expresses the freedom, strength and radicalism of the building's inhabitants (students of the three disciplines represented here). The use of colour, then, was seen as an instrument to allow the students to "own" the project, allowing them to identify with a contemporary attitude that, at the same time, is capable of cohabitating with the historical urban fabric.

04

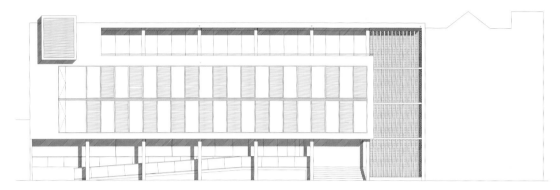

01 Main staircase **02** Courtyard of the architecture, art and design building **03** Library entrance, 2nd level **04** Elevation **05** Section **06** Auditorium, 2nd level **07** Inner courtyard, 4th floor

05

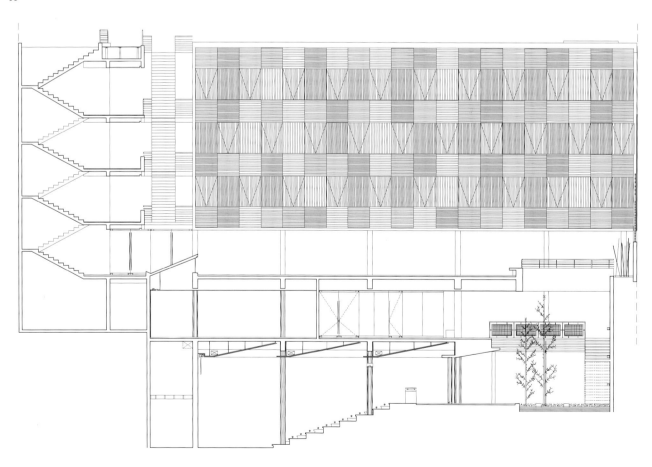

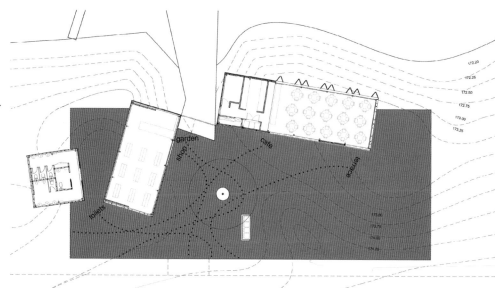

Welcome Mat, Mount Penang, Australia, 2003
Entry facilities to the park comprising restaurant, shop, ticket office, toilets
Address: Mount Penang, Kariong, Gosford NSW, Australia. **Landscape architect:** Anton James Design. **Client:** Festival Development Corporation. **Gross floor area:** café: 108 m²; shop: 72 m²; toilets: 36 m²; total: 216 m². **Materials:** steel frame construction with 4 different façades: printed vinyl, timber screen, reinforcement mesh with planting, mirror.

Welcome Mat
ARCHITECTS: Lacoste + Stevenson

Mt. Penang Gardens are public gardens located on the central coast of Australia, one hour's drive north of Sydney. The entrance buildings are placed, seemingly at random, on a red bitumen "Welcome Mat". This defines the space upon which the entrance buildings are located and clearly marks the entrance as warm and inviting. The mat takes the form of the gently undulating landform in a way that a carpet would when placed on the ground. The striking red welcomes visitors to the garden and is complemented by the vinyl supergraphic of red grevillia on one of the building façades, a plant native to the area. The graphic and planted façades, as viewed on approaching the garden, make playful use of colour and materials in anticipation of the garden itself. This contrasts with the view of the façades from the garden across the water; mirror and timber slats dematerialise the buildings, reducing their presence.

01 Plan **02** Exterior view **03** Entrance **04** Exterior view

01

Sheraton Abandoibarra Hotel Bilbao, 2004
Address: Bilbao, Spain. **Associate architect:** TDM
Arquitectos. **Floor area:** 193,000 sq.ft.

Close to Gehry
ARCHITECTS: LEGORRETA + LEGORRETA

This hotel is part of the new "Ria 2000" master plan
for the City of Bilbao. It is located several blocks from
the Guggenheim Museum. The hotel was designed as a
compact volume in harmony with the surrounding environment. Inspired by the work of artist Eduardo Chillida
and the history and culture of the Basque Country, the
building is treated like a stone block that is transformed
into a perforated "sculpture". In its interior there is an
eight-storey central atrium that culminates in a half-
vaulted ceiling. Light plays a very important role in this
space as it is illuminated by the different perforations,
creating a different game of light and shadow at each
hour of the day. The façade is treated like a lattice window with nine squares per room to provide maximum
intimacy for residents while ensuring that the façade
forms a single massive form.

02

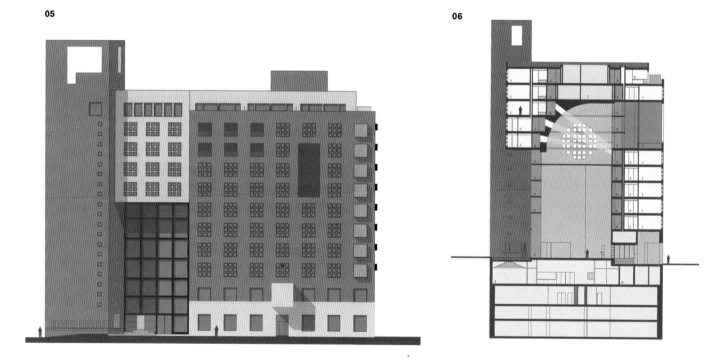

01 Business centre **02** Main façade **03** Central atrium **04** Typical
floor **05** Elevation **06** Section **07**
Terrace bar

1. BEDROOMS
2. HALLWAY
3. EXECUTIVE SUITE

0 1m 2m   5m   10m   15m

05

06

Casa en La Florida, 2006
Address: La Florida near Madrid, Spain.

Silicon house

ARCHITECTS: selgascano
José Selgas and Lucía Cano

The house is built on a slight incline, in an idyllic setting surrounded by holm oak, ash, acacia and pine. It enters into a dialogue with this stunningly beautiful sanctuary of nature, perched on two platforms and under two slightly curved flat roofs. These have been designed in two contrasting colours and fitted with bubble-like skylights. There is a lot of light in this house thanks to the extensive glazing. The interior floor covering is made of soft recycled rubber and the rooms are furnished with cushioned plastic benches and stools in a variety of organic shapes. These continue the dialogue with the exterior environment, with trees planted in special niches. The villa makes clever use of the cover provided by this vegetation, blending into the topography and thereby giving rise to a variety of interior.

01

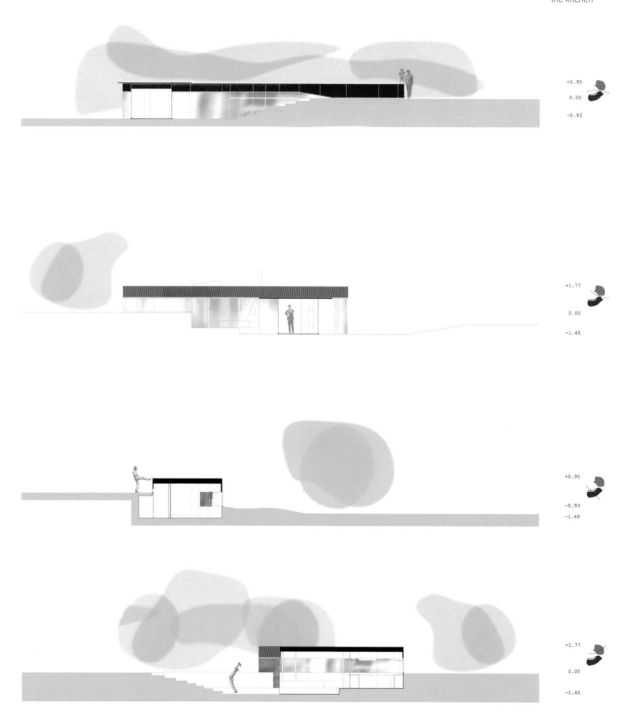

+0.95
0.00
-0.93

+1.77
0.00
-1.40

+0.95
-0.93
-1.68

+1.77
0.00
-1.40

BROWN

ORANGE

YELLOW

The Copenhagen Opera, 2004
Address: Ekvipagemestervej 10, 1438 Copenhagen K, Denmark. **Acoustics:** Arup Acoustics (UK). **Engineering:** Rambøll in collaboration with Buro Happold (UK). **Lighting design:** Speirs and Major Associates (UK). **Client:** The A.P. Møller and Chastine MC-Kinney Møller Foundation. **Gross floor area:** 41,000 m². **Materials:** sandstone, granite, metal and glass.

Precious string instrument
ARCHITECTS: Henning Larsen Architects A/S, Copenhagen

The Copenhagen Opera is located at a unique and beautiful site in the central harbour of Copenhagen opposite the Royal Castle. The façades of the main building are covered with Jura Yellow natural stone, the attractive, smooth surface broken by bands of windows and narrow lighting slots. This contrasts with the open foyer facing the harbour, whose walls are mainly of glass, the natural stone surface of the plaza and the metal roof. The design of the auditorium ensures comfort, an excellent view of the stage and state-of-the-art acoustics. Moreover, it contributes to the opera's expansive ambience; the auditorium holds 1,400 visitors on two levels of stalls and three balconies. The balconies are covered on the inside and outside in wood treated in the same manner as precious string instruments. The materials and colours were mainly chosen from the lighter end of the colour scale in order to relate to the surroundings and to adhere to the simple Nordic tradition in architecture.

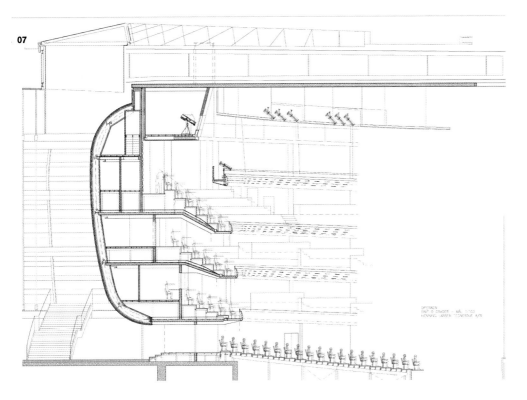

07

08

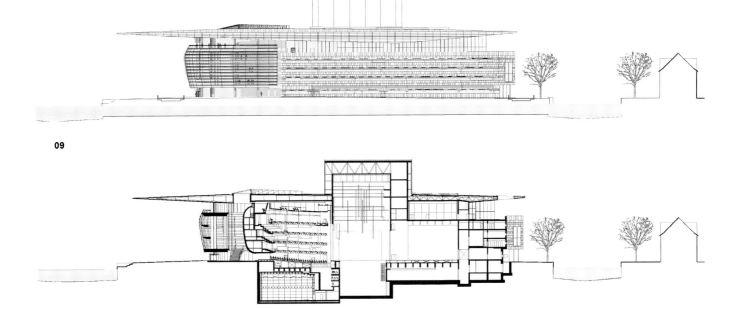

09

1970s housing estate in Strucksbarg, Hamburg
Address: Strucksbarg 39–55, In der Alten Forst 1a–e,
21077 Hamburg, Germany. **Client:** Grundstücksge-
meinschaft Martens, Per Schumann Immobilien KG,
Wolfram Schumann-Plekat. **Façade surface:**
3,685.34 m². **Materials:** thermal insulation composite
system, plaster, steel, glass, natural stone.

Provocation in colour
ARCHITECTS: Renner Hainke Wirth
Architekten, Hamburg

The Strucksbarg housing complex in Wilhelmsburg was
built in the 1970s – not a good time for residential architecture. It has now benefited from some lasting im-
provements and been made fit for the future. After un-
dergoing asbestos abatement and receiving additional
thermal insulation, the next step was to provide something for the eye to savour. Powerful colour accents
ranging from yellow to dark red embellish the simple façades. It is particularly the elements that stand out that
receive the benefit of striking colour markings: red, orange and yellow for the entrances, balcony balustrades
and balcony partitions. Colour is used as a means to
fetch, awaken, and provoke the residents out of their
anonymity. The attempt has succeeded.

01 Site plan **02** Façade tower block **03** Entrance

03

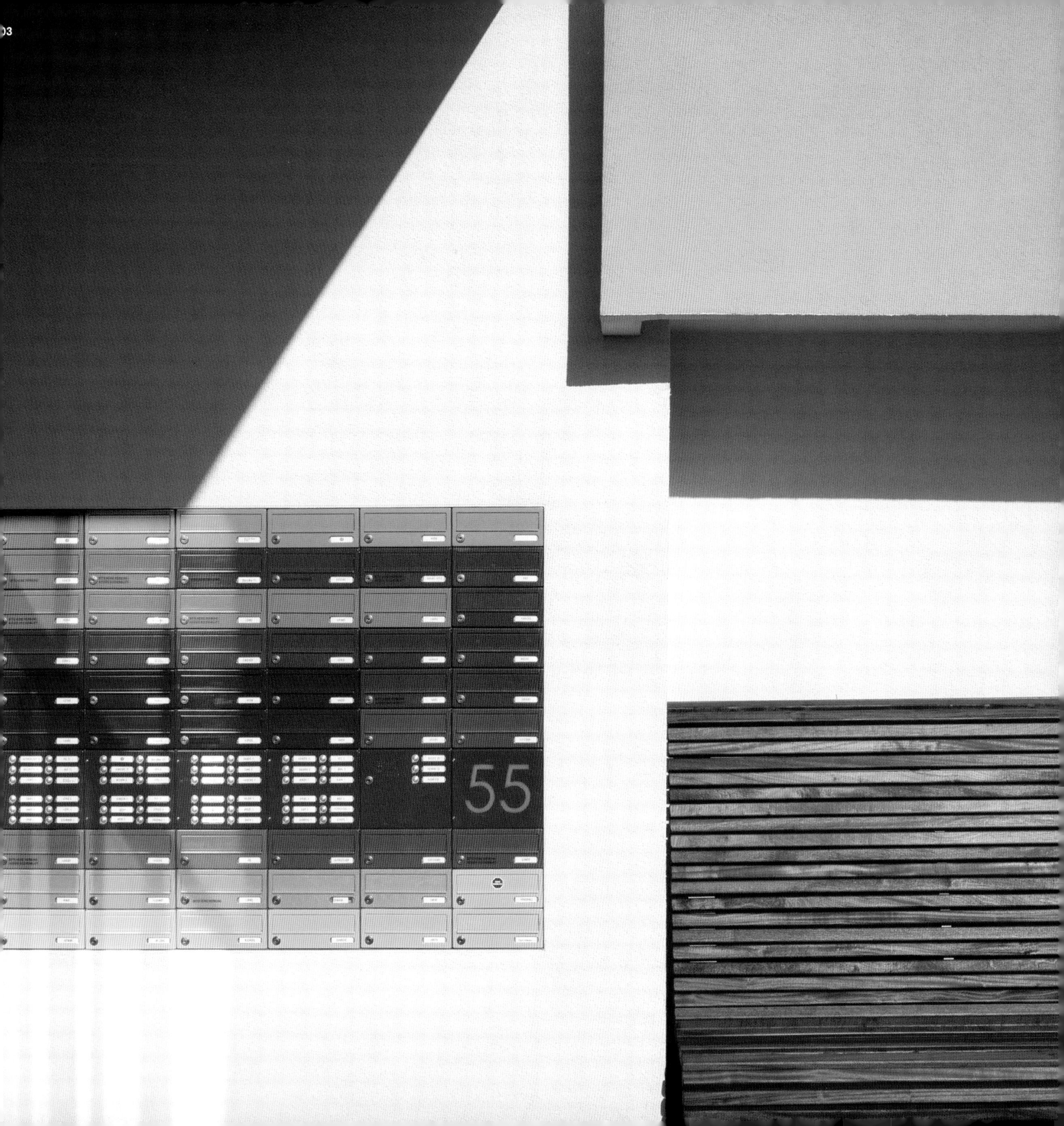

Seewürfel / Seewurfel, 2005
Residential and commercial buildings
Address: Seefeldstrasse 277, 8008 Zurich, Switzerland. **Client:** Swiss Life. **Gross floor area:** 12,000 m².
Materials: wood, glass.

A human ambience of lightness
ARCHITECTS: Camenzind Evolution
Architecture – Design – Technology, Zurich

The eight new apartment and office buildings are situated close to the town centre of Zurich and offer stunning views of the lake and surrounding cityscape. This project regenerates a former industrial site as an attractive new centre for working and living and fits harmoniously into the existing historic fabric of the area. Seewurfel (literally 'Lake Cubes') is based on a piazza design created by the deliberate positioning of the eight buildings. The individually landscaped piazzas and external spaces create a variety of different environments to be used and enjoyed by Seewurfel occupants and their neighbours. The strong colour and texture of the timber-glass panels, together with the soft, moving reflections on the glass, create a human ambience of lightness and warmth in the piazzas between the buildings.

04

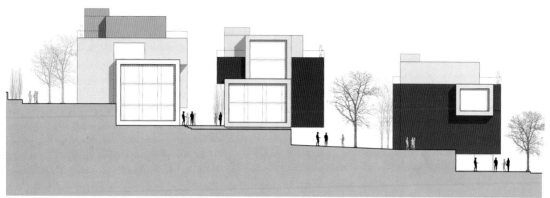

05

Studio
Study
31.0 m2

Zimmer
Room
20.0 m2

Zimmer
Room
48.0 m2

Studio
Study
40.0 m2

01

Youth hostel in Bremen, 2005
Address: Kalkstrasse 6, 28195 Bremen, Germany.
Client: German Youth Hostel Association (DJH)
Unterweser-Ems. **Gross floor area:** 4,076 m².
Materials: structure: reinforced concrete, masonry
(old building); façades: cube – rear ventilated, point-
mounted enamelled glass panels, alternating with cus-
tom aluminium window frames applied to aluminium
windows, base – Alucobond cladding.

Yellow signs
ARCHITECTS: raumzeit

The youth hostel in Bremen is an important element
in the city's revitalisation of its waterfront and the surrounding Faulenquartier district. A prestige project for
the German Youth Hostel Association, the hostel is
fully booked nearly all year. The building, conceived as
a composition of slab, cube and base, is clad in façades
of different materials and colours. The aubergine tone
of the base is evocative of the reddish brown brick of
the existing building but is highly glossy, not matt and
porous like the bricks. The dark colour makes the bright
yellow tones of the new dormitory shine by contrast.
Together, the dark aubergine and the yellow tones produce varying effects under different light conditions and
sight angles. Within the cityscape, the building always
shines in the distance like a powerful, vivid signal – similar to the yellow navigation signs that stand along the
Weser river.

02

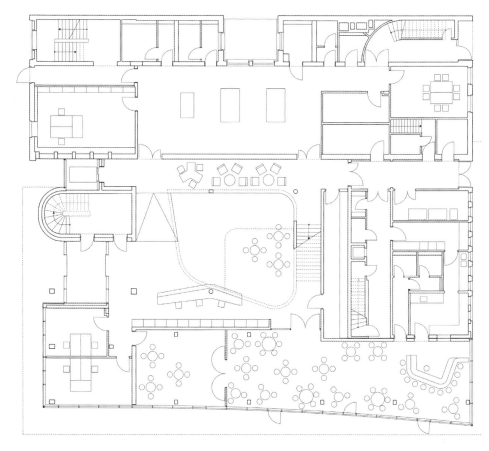

01 The hostel as landmark on the waterfront **02** Floor plan street level
03 Terrace from the west

3

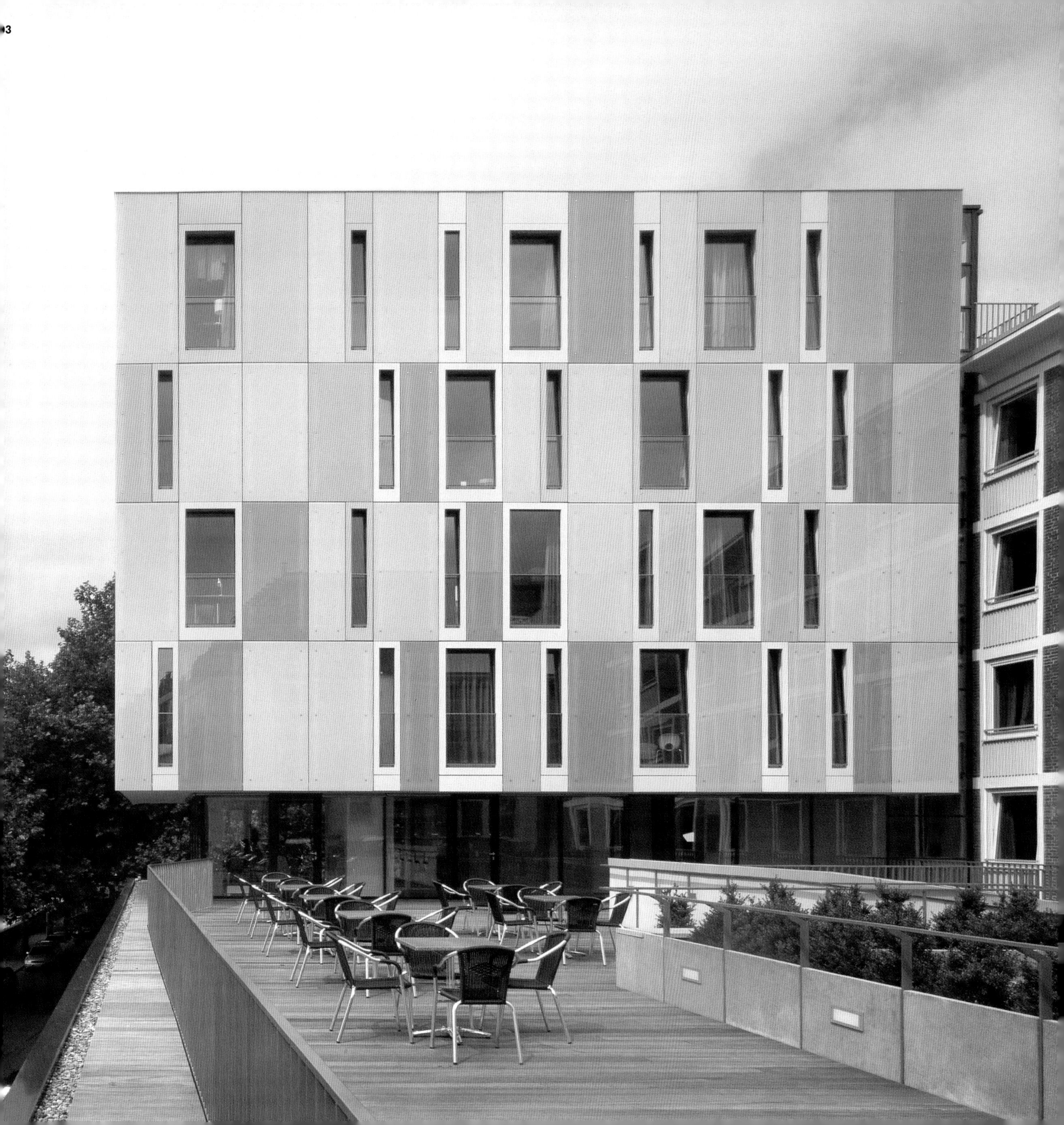

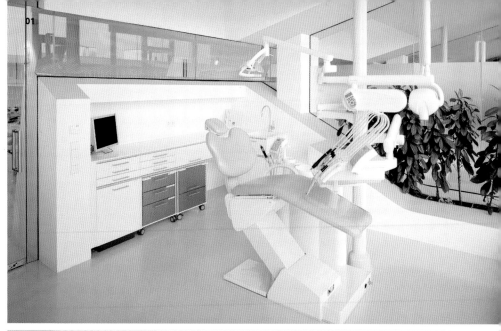

Dentist's practice KU64, 2005
Address: Kurfürstendamm 64, 10707 Berlin, Germany.
Planner: DEMEDIS Dental-Depot GmbH. **Support-**
ing structure: K55 Dipl.-Ing. K+T Gehlhaar. **Gross**
floor area: 940 m². **Materials:** Knauf dry construction
systems.

On the beach

ARCHITECTS: GRAFT Lars Krückeberg,
Wolfram Putz, Thomas Willemeit, Berlin

The very thought of a dentist's practice evokes an image of hygiene and sterility, the everlasting monologue
of white, not to mention the unmistakable odour. But
everything is different here. The image evoked is that of
a landscape of dunes in which the beach visitor seeks
a spot in the sand, lays out his towel and gazes off into
the distance. It is a room in which the floor warps up-
ward and the ceiling forms waves. The arrangement of
dune summits and valleys preserves privacy and fosters
intimacy while allowing a generously open view through
the entire practice. The floor, which folds to form waves
and merges with walls, has a striking orange surface
consisting of four layers: colourless spray elastomers, a
coloured seal, anamorphic motifs as white rasters, and
a final transparent seal.

04

05

06

07

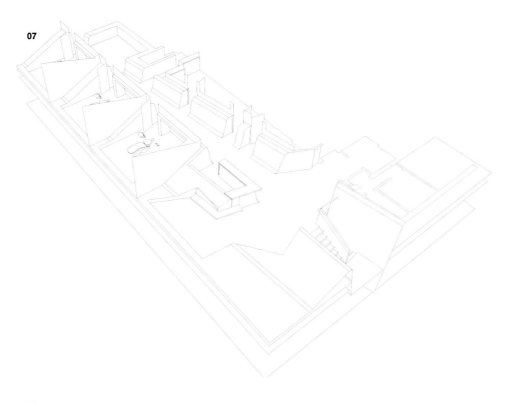

08

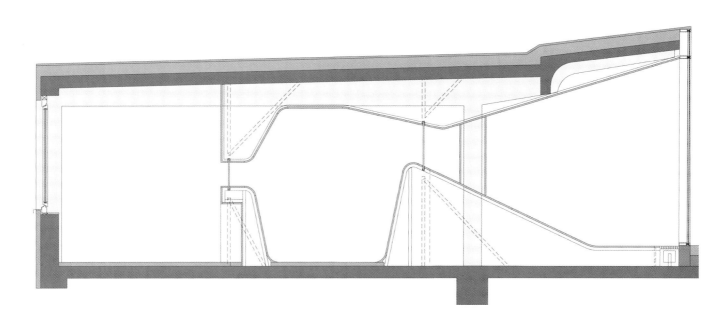

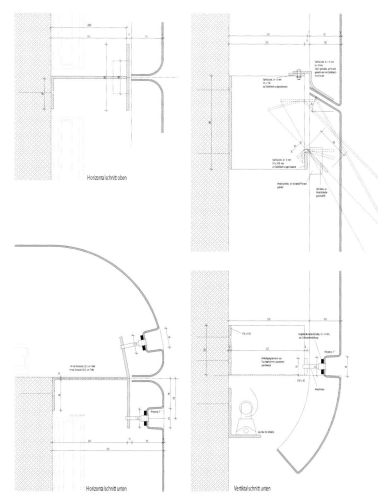

Gas transfer station, Dachau, 2004
Address: Schleißheimer Straße, 85221 Dachau, Germany. **Client:** Dachau Municipal Works. **Materials:** glassfibre-reinforced plastic.

A meaningful façade
ARCHITECTS: dv Architekten

The banal concrete form of a gas transfer station located near former palaces of the Bavarian monarchy at Schleissheim and Dachau has been draped in translucent GRP, a material that has rarely been used in façade construction yet has the advantages of being strong but lightweight and heavily resistant to chemicals and weather conditions. The motif on this membrane, facing outwards, depicts the machinery within the station. The printer's copy was a 360° photograph. The motif is visible both in reflected and transmitted light. An extra effect is achieved here by the fact that the motif not only clings to the surface, but is deeply impregnated like a tattoo. Between the concrete shell and the GRP sheath there is a gap of 30 to 40 cm that is evenly illuminated at night by neon strip lights. This lighting switches on automatically with the street lights. The façade conveys text, symbolism and meaning. One can read it; it communicates with its surroundings.

01 View from the south east by night **02** Details **03** View from the north east **04** Detail

02

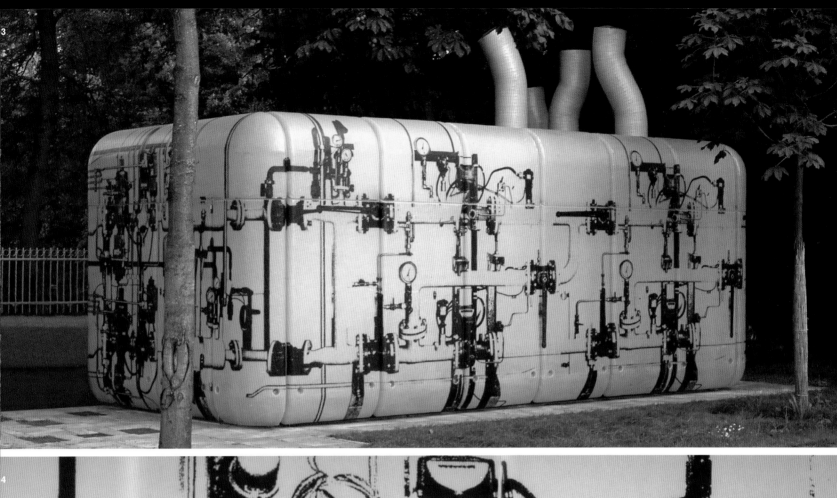

House on the square, 2004
Address: Mirabeauweg 1, 72072 Tübingen, Germany.
Client: Bauherrengemeinschaft Haus am Platz. **Gross floor area:** 1,560 m² (residential space 767 m², commercial space 94 m²). **Materials:** reinforced concrete, chalky sandstone, composite thermal insulation system, wooden window frames.

Two in one
ARCHITECTS: LEHEN drei
Architekten Stadtplaner BDA SRL
Martin Feketics Leonhard Schenk
Matthias Schuster

The basic idea behind this project is to divide a building into separate dwelling and sleeping wings. While the sleeping wing is screened by a classic punctuated façade of narrow windows, the dwelling wing is extensively glazed on its west- and east-facing ends. The sleeping wing houses the common starcase and lift in addition to the bedrooms and bathrooms. From the stairs one enters the "joint" between the two buildings. This lobby-like intermediary space is fully glazed at both ends. The sleeping wing also has its own entrance hall that can be closed off with a door. The dwelling wing opens expansively onto the "joining" area and contains the living, dining and cooking areas. The building's overall colour scheme emphasises the differing characters of the two tower-like structures. The sleeping wing is painted a calm, warming yellow while the dwelling wing in which most of the daily activities take place is a rich and powerful red.

01 3rd floor plan **02** View from north east **03** View from west

Theatre Agora, 2007
Theatre and Congress Centre
Address: Agorabaan 12, 8224 JS Lelystad, The Netherlands. **Client:** Municipality of Lelystad. **Gross floor area:** 7,000 m². **Materials:** steel, concrete, aluminium, glass, acoustic panelling.

01

Kaleidoscopic experience
ARCHITECTS: Ben van Berkel / UNStudio

The Agora Theatre is an extremely colourful, determinedly upbeat place. The building is part of the master plan for Lelystad by Adriaan Geuze, which aims to revitalize the pragmatic, sober town centre. Both interior and exterior walls are designed to reflect the kaleidoscopic experience of the world of the stage, where you can never be sure of what is real and what is not. In the Agora Theatre drama and performance are not restricted to the stage and to the eveningtime, but extend to the urban experience and to daytime. Inside, the colourfulness of the exterior is exceeded in intensity; a handrail designed as a snaking pink ribbon cascades down the main staircase, winds itself all around the void at the centre of the large, open foyer space on the first floor and then extends up the wall towards the roof, changing colour all the while from violet, crimson and cherry to almost white. The main theatre is all in red.

02

04

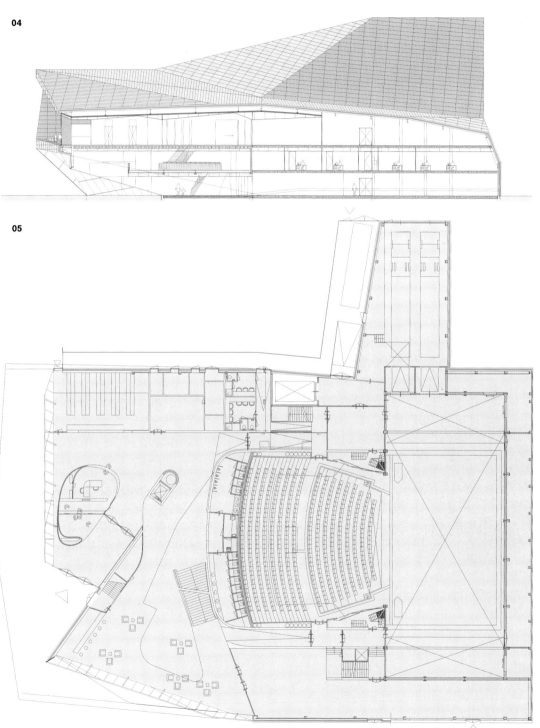

05

01 Exterior façade, west **02** Interior, foyer **03** Exterior façade, south **04** Section **05** Floor plan, Level 0 **06** Interior, Main Hall

70

06

House in San Miguel de Allende, 2005
Address: San Miguel de Allende, Guanajuato, Mexico.
Associate architect: Ignacio Pastor. **Floor area:**
6,890 sq.ft.

Under the tree
ARCHITECTS: LEGORRETA + LEGORRETA

The façade facing Aldama street was designed taking into consideration the strict rules of the INAH (National Institute of Anthropology and History). The main concern was not to break with the general milieu of the city centre, conserving the proportions of windows, heights and colours. A very important tree existed on the lot, and the project was developed around this tree, creating a courtyard as the focal point of the house. The access corridor takes the form of a pathway around the courtyard, surrounded by lattice windows with vertical elements that let one discreetly view the tree and the terrace and creating a sensation of mystery. The courtyard is surrounded by the access corridor, the kitchen, the living room and the dining room. It thus becomes the centre of a play of light and shade and water. The studio and the social area, including an open living room, also have a magnificent view of the terrace, garden and pool.

01 The house from the garden **02** The dining room from the upstairs corridor **03** "Patio" (courtyard) with a red onix outdoor table **04** Plan **05** Stairs to the second floor, next to a ramp where waters run from top to bottom

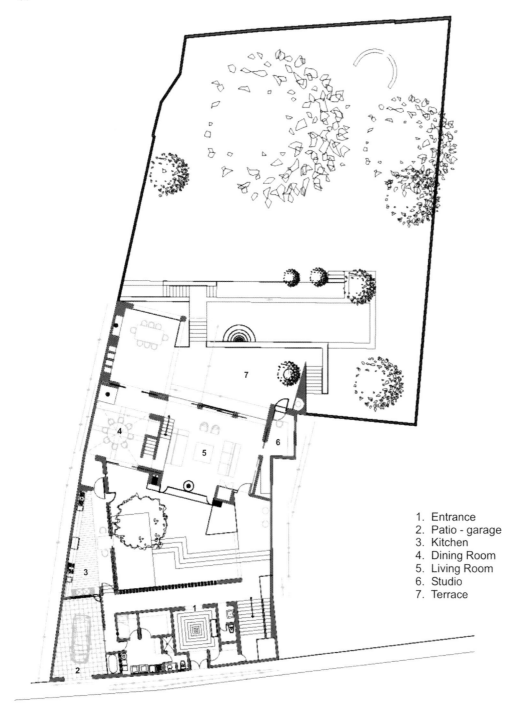

7

4

5

6

3

1

2

1. Entrance
2. Patio - garage
3. Kitchen
4. Dining Room
5. Living Room
6. Studio
7. Terrace

The Disney Store Headquarters, 2007
Address: Pasadena, California. **Client:** The Children's Place. **Gross floor area:** 7,525 m².

Mickey Mouse ears
ARCHITECTS: Clive Wilkinson Architects

The original wood framed building is composed of three parts. The front portion is a 4.9-metre-high space with large timber trusses. The large rear portion is a double height wooden framed atrium space with a saw-tooth roof, creating dramatic clerestory lighting that spans the width of the space. These two portions are connected by a long interstitial brick walled structure, which inspired the creation of brick-like elements for the interior. These modular elements allude to children's block building games and remind staff of their role in creating products for children. In addition to providing an internal landscaped courtyard and new skylights throughout, the building also connects occupants to the exterior with a new landscaped courtyard at the front. This includes an ivy topiary of "Mickey Mouse ears". Most days the doors to the interior courtyard, which is accessed from the cafeteria, are left open, allowing fresh air and sunlight to permeate the space.

04

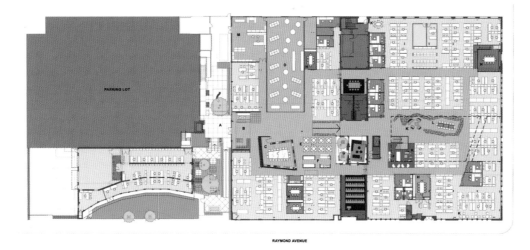

PARKING LOT

RAYMOND AVENUE

01 Rear atrium, open workstations, "honeycomb conference room" **02** "Block conference room" – stacked **03** "Block conference room" – unstacked **04** First floor plan **05** 3-D rendering **06** Rear atrium, workstations, "honeycomb conference room"

05

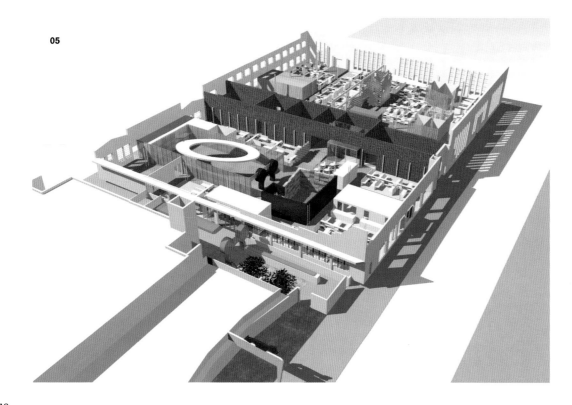

6

Signage system with service pavilions for the Volkspark Potsdam, 2005
Address: Potsdam, Germany. **Client:** Entwicklungsträger Bornstedter Feld GmbH. **Gross floor area of information pavilions:** 11.9 m². **Materials:** cladding: orange Alucobond panels; graphics: film cut in white/grey.

Potsdam's man-made landscape
ARCHITECTS: Wiechers Beck Architekten

This project involved designing an information and orientation system for the Volkspark in Potsdam. The uniform design plan for pictograms, signs and buildings is characterised by the way it contrasts with the park's design. The independence of the objects is emphasized by the artificial colours and comic-like depiction of recognisable symbols. Corresponding to the organisation of the park into accessible areas, an elaborate system of paths is also provided, consisting of one main path and five "trails". At each intersection an information pavilion provides the visitor with information about the park and Potsdam's cultural landscape. A powerful orange was chosen as the basic colour for these information pavilions, while a moderate, friendly green on a neutral white background was chosen for the other elements of the orientation system.

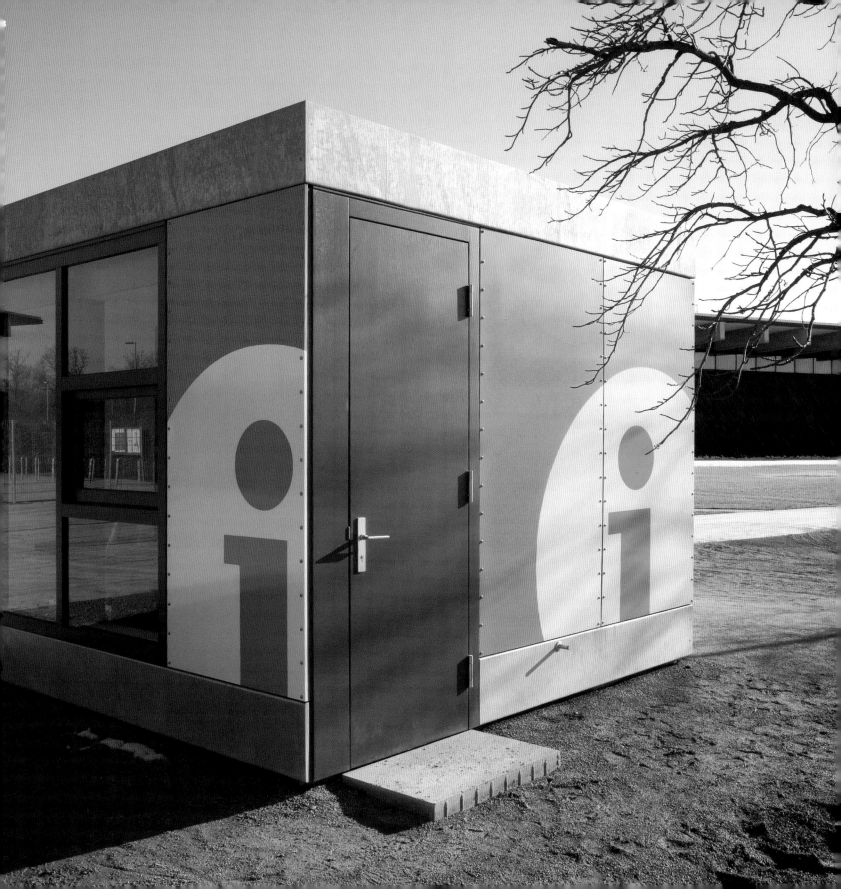

04

01 Detail WC pavilion **02** WC pavilion, southern view **03** Information pavilion, northern view **04** Overview orientation system **05** WC pavilion, south western view

leitsystem volkspark I gesamtkonzept 1

GRILLPLATZ

GREEN

BLUE

Urban planning design "Smolni", 2007
Address: Kalininski Administrative District, on the site of the former "Rossiya" factory, St. Petersburg, Russia. **Gross floor area:** 368,685 m².

Homage to Benois
ARCHITECTS: Sergei Tchoban
nps tchoban voss GbR Architekten BDA
A. M. Prasch P. Sigl S. Tchoban E. Voss

Where the former gardens of the Kuschelev-Besborodko mansion border today's Piskarevski Prospect is where the house of the Russian artist Alexandre Benois once stood. This site is now filled by a partially derelict industrial building. It is planned to redevelop this building and convert it to a multifunctional business centre. The design of the new building will be dedicated to Benois, particularly to his work in the theatre which, through his collaboration with Sergei Diaghilev, helped to bring Russian art and theatre to world attention. Benois' sketches for theatre costumes form the basis for the digital figurine prints on the glass of the front façade. The storey-high printed glass is set in an aluminium post-and-beam construction, which spans the entire facade as a supporting structure.

01 View from the street 02 Rear view 03 Detail façade with back-lit figures 04 Section 05 Site plan 06 Detail façade

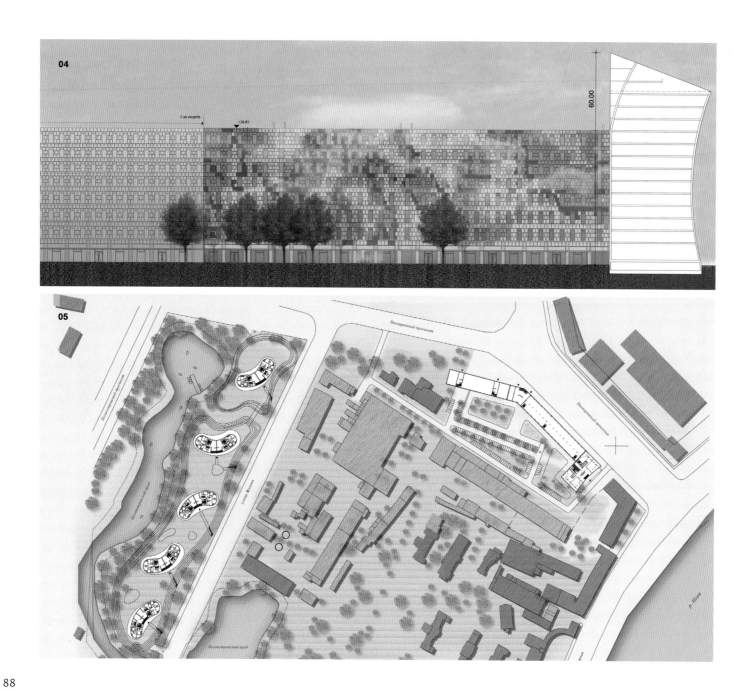

04

05

01

Mensa Moltke – university canteen, 2007
Address: Moltkestrasse 12, Karlsruhe, Germany.
Client: Baden-Wuerttemberg State Authority for Property and Construction, Karlsruhe office. **User:** Studentenwerk Karlsruhe. **Gross floor area:** 3,008 m². **Material/paints:** RAL 6022 (olive drab) for the frames of all façade windows and doors, RAL 1000 (green beige) for the walls and ceilings of the timber structure, and RAL 6019 (pastel green) for all solid elements.

A mirror image of the forest
ARCHITECTS: J. MAYER H.

The new canteen is a functionally and formally flexible space that is situated at the centre of the university campus in Karlsruhe and links the three existing universities, the neighbouring built-up area, and the adjoining Hardt Forest. It almost seems as though the façade were intended to mirror the structure of a German forest (deutscher Wald). The powerful concrete columns rise in random and oblique disorder. The building reacts to its environment with various layers of permeability. Reflecting the transition from Hardt Forest to city, the "forest" theme has also been worked into the green-brown colour design of the interior. This colour choice has been complemented by the furniture with its spectrum of green tones. The interplay of these colours creates a warm and lively atmosphere, but one that also has a certain tension – comparable to the green shimmer in a painting by Cezanne.

02

07

08

01 Dining area **02** Patio **03** Main façade Moltkestrasse **04** Side view gallery **05** Gallery **06** Staircase gallery **07** Ground floor plan **08** Upper floor plan **09** Model MKA idea

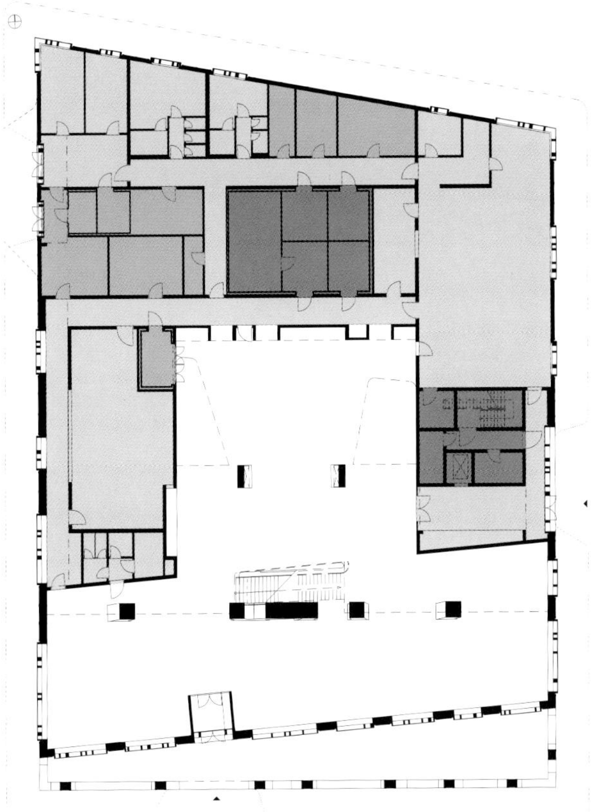

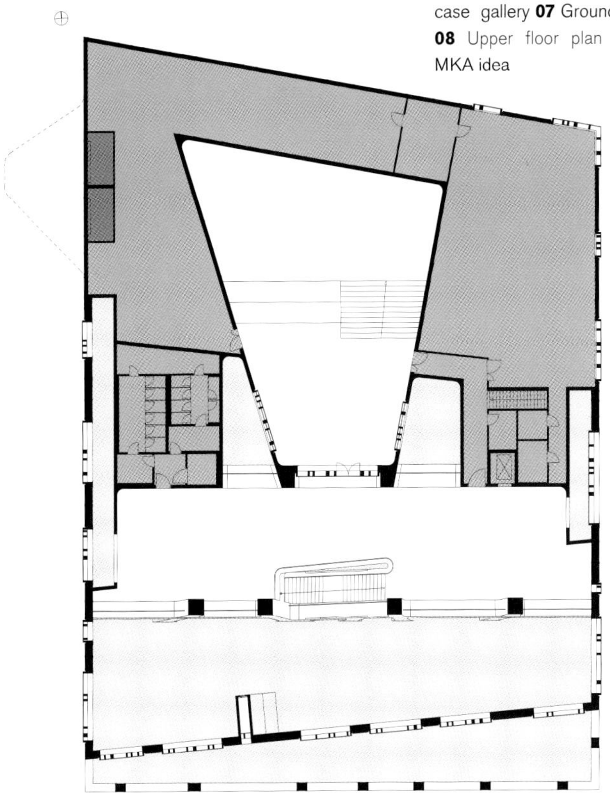

09

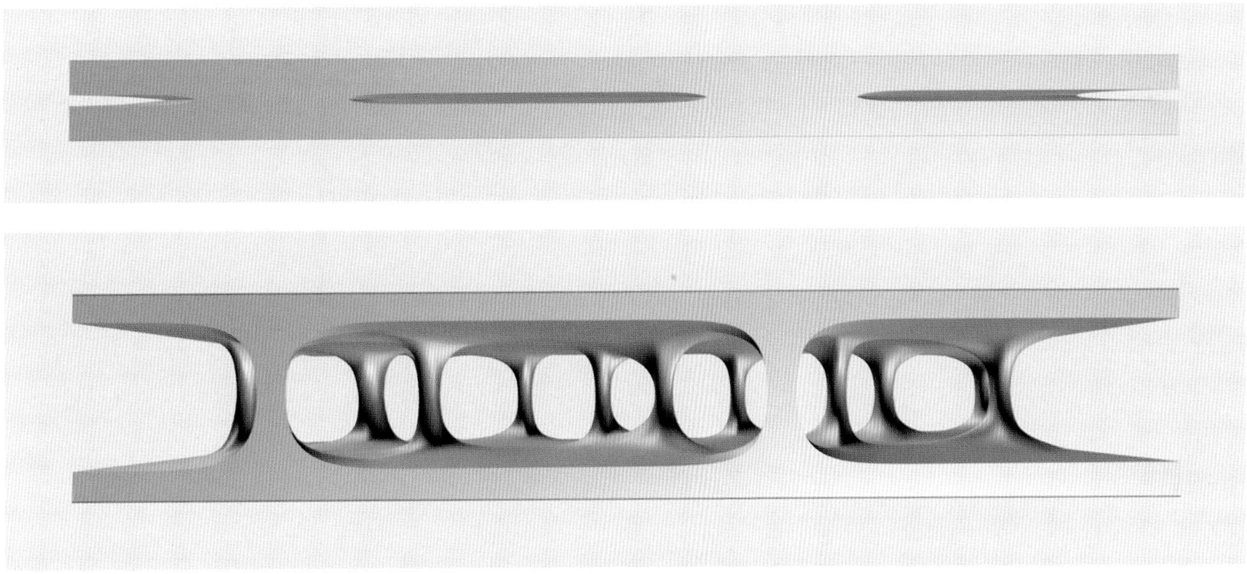

Residential apartments overlooking community plaza in Düsseldorf-Gerresheim, 2006
Address: Heinrich-Könn-Str. 60a–I, 40625 Düsseldorf-Gerresheim, Germany. **Client:** antes... Immobilien GmbH. **Gross floor area:** 2,615 m². **Materials:** rendered façade, aluminium and wooden windows, larchwood timbering.

Raspberry red and lime green
ARCHITECTS: Atelier Fritschi Stahl Baum, Düsseldorf

The apartment complex and community plaza are the last modules in a larger residential development. The distinctive lime green tower marks the entrance to the complex. The textured surface of the façade produces fine nuances of colour and emphasises the tower's function as the entrance building. The raspberry red main block contains eight narrow triplex townhouses (4-metre clear width) and is separated from the tower by a covered passage. Unlike the street frontage with its informally arranged windows, the façade with its larchwood loggias facing the plaza is fully glazed. Small courtyards as well as patios and balconies on the upper floors create a kind of "vertical garden".

01 Tower on the entrance of the complex **02** Façade facing the plaza
03 Intermediate zone between tower and main block

01

Idea Store Whitechapel, London, 2005
Library and learning centre
Address: 319 Whitechapel Road, London, E1 1BU, United Kingdom. **Client:** London Borough of Tower Hamlets. **Gross floor area:** 3440 m². **Materials:** laminated green, blue and clear glass, concrete, perforated steel, laminated veneer lumber, wood fibre board, spruce plywood, red rubber flooring.

Inspired by the market
ARCHITECTS: Adjaye / Associates, London

The Idea Store Whitechapel is the flagship building of a programme based on a new type of information and learning provision being pioneered by the London Borough of Tower Hamlets. Each will combine the resources of a modern library with walk-in access to a range of taught courses for people of all ages from across the community. The Idea Store Whitechapel integrates educational spaces with information facilities and other resources including a dance studio and a complementary therapies space. Internally, the exposed concrete frame defines a series of zones, which feel welcoming and inclusive. The design of light fittings, bookshelves and worktops create an intimate and flexible environment capable of responding to a wide range of needs. The materiality and range of colour used for the building are inspired by the nearby market stalls whose framed superstructures are draped in green and blue striped sheets.

04

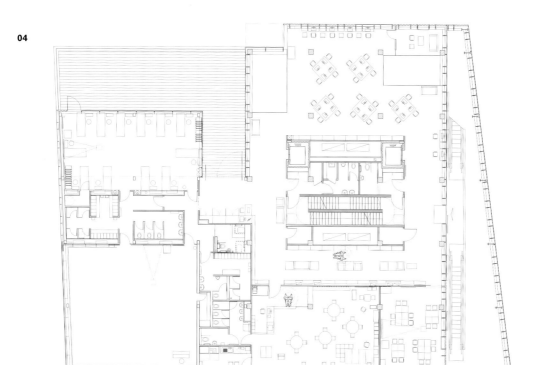

01 Looking towards the City on Whitechapel Road 02 Looking west towards City 03 Night view, south façade 04 First floor plan 05 South elevation 06 Looking down onto Whitechapel Road 07 Façade

05

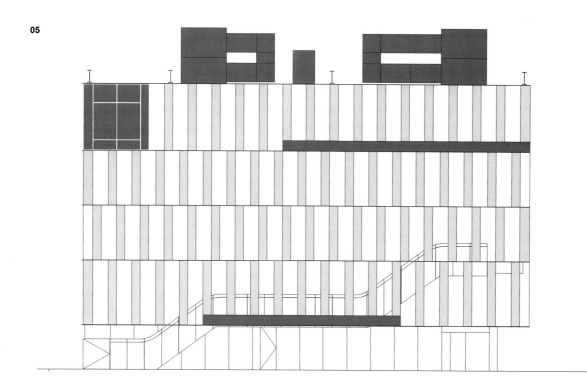

Eching Middle School (Realschule), 2006
Address: Untere Hauptstraße 3, 85386 Eching, Germany. **Colour scheme:** Herbert Kopp, Munich. **Client:** District of Freising, Freising District Administration. **Gross floor area:** 12,629 m². **Materials:** aluminium slatted blinds; walls fitted with composite thermal insulation; mineral finish coat; balcony screens of powder-coated aluminium sheeting; windows in powder-coated wood and aluminium; rubber flooring.

A new whole – with colour
ARCHITECTS: Diezinger & Kramer
Dipl. Inge Architekten BDA

This school building owes its visual impact to its use of colour. It seems to draw attention to the fact that it is a public building. The bold use of colour continues in the interior, bathing corridors and classrooms in a soft, multicoloured light that changes continually throughout the day. The role of colour in architecture is not merely as a decorative element. Rather, it adds an emotional and atmospheric dimension – in this case turning a school building into an expressive and memorable space. Like in Renaissance or Baroque architecture, colour is understood here as an integral component of the architecture. Areas of colour are not designed in a purely tectonic way (i.e., emphasising the architectural elements) but rather "artistically". The interplay of colour and space thus gives birth to a new "whole".

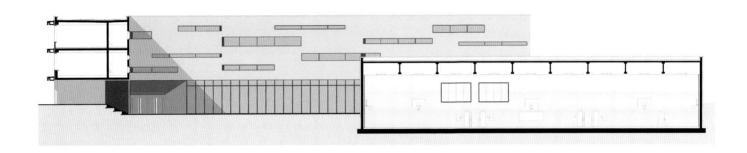

08

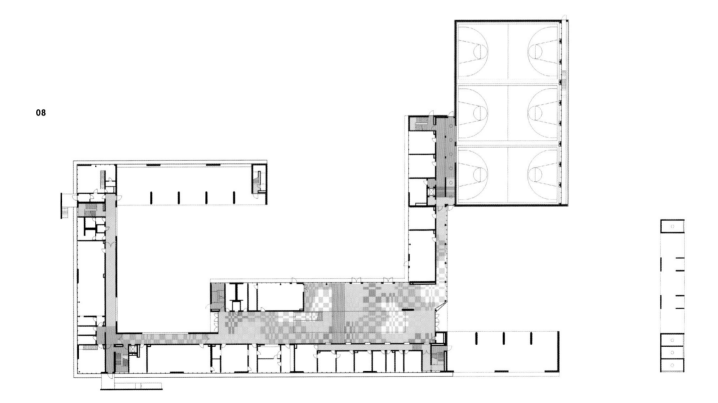

Käthe-Kollwitz-School in Darmstadt, 2004
Address: Koblenzer Straße 8, 64293 Darmstadt, Germany. **Building art:** Florian Baudrexel. **Client:** City of Darmstadt represented by the Public Building and Mechanics Authority. **Gross floor area:** 1,044 m². **Materials:** reinforced concrete, both cast in situ and precast, masonry for interior walls, glass/aluminium for windows and façades.

Relaunch or: the modern form of a precast concrete school

ARCHITECTS: P. Karle / R. Buxbaum
Freie Architekten · Diplom Ingenieure

This project involved an extension of five new classrooms and several storerooms to a primary school that was built in the 1970s. The existing building was originally constructed with precast concrete which is today, following several alteration measures in the interior, still in good condition. Consequently, when it came to extending the building the precast concrete units were used only as a structural frame into which the body shell of wood and glass was placed. The Düsseldorf artist Florian Baudrexel developed the ideas for his art project and the school's colour scheme based on the visual world of children in the 1970s and the spirograph painting toy that was popular at that time. Details of a spirograph line drawing, greatly enlarged in scale and extending up to the second floor, form the motif for the design of the corridor walls which function as a green guide wall in the interior and dominate the exterior view from the schoolyard.

04

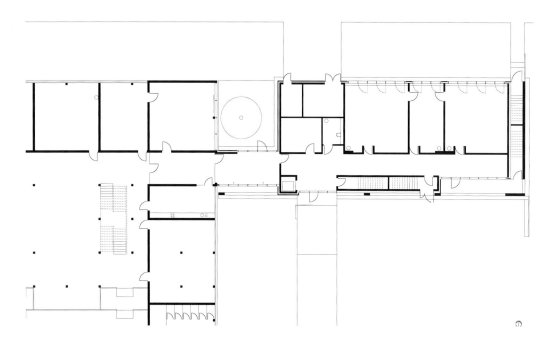

05

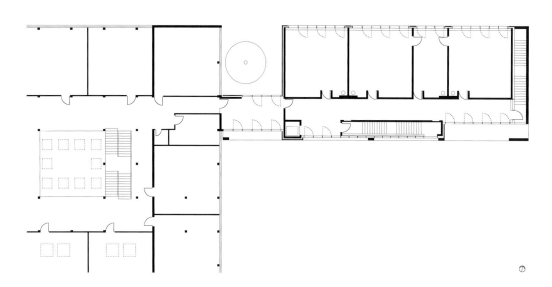

01 View of the extension from the schoolyard **02** Classroom on the upper floor with view on the spirograph wall painting **03** Hallway on the upper floor with spirograph wall painting and green guide wall **04** Ground floor plan **05** Upper floor plan **06** Staircase

06

Temporary Hamburg Cruise Centre, HafenCity, 2004
Address: Am Grasbrookhafen 1, 20457 Hamburg, Germany. **Structural planning:** Werner Sobek, Ingenieurbüro im Bauwesen GmbH, Stuttgart. **Client:** HafenCity Hamburg GmbH. **Gross floor area:** 1,500 m². **Materials:** containers, steel and glass construction, timber framing, insulated sheet metal sandwich roof.

Light, materiality and colour

ARCHITECTS: Renner Hainke Wirth
Architekten, Hamburg

Only four months were available from awarding of the contract to its completion. New security regulations and the visit of the Queen Mary II to Hamburg were the factors that inspired and set the date for the completion of this system of containers that comprises the cruise terminal. Fifty-one used containers were taken from Hamburg port and painted in a variety of colours. The necessary changes for door and window openings were undertaken on site at the port. The construction of the container walls took a mere eight hours. The containers are painted in iridescent maritime blue and green to contrast the orange floor in the interior. The roof consists of a protruding structural framework that is somewhat reminiscent of the age of sailing ships (i.e. sails). Also part of the ensemble is a HafenCity View-Point platform in a distinctive yellow-orange tone that provides a horizontal counterpoint to the main structure. The orthogonal structure of the growing city is framed by the organic shaped windows.

2

03

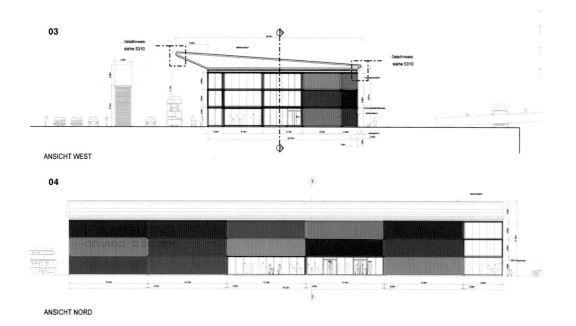

ANSICHT WEST

04

ANSICHT NORD

01 ViewPoint with city panorama **02** Cruise terminal entrance and west elevation **03** West elevation with light pipe in front of the terminal **04** North elevation **05** Floor plan **06** View from the city

05

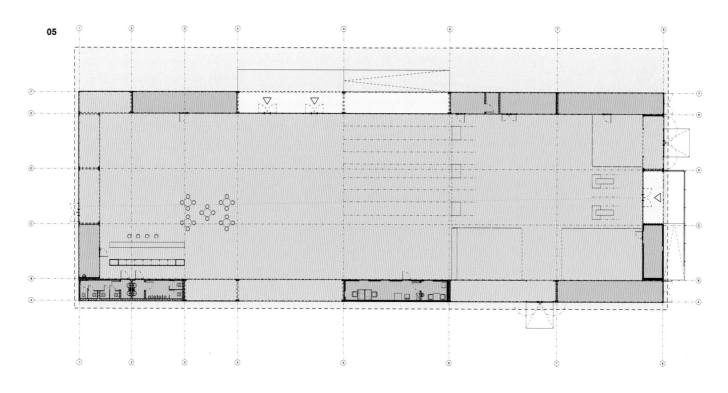

01

Façade design of the High Tech Park,
Heavy Industry Zone, Lingang, China, 2007
Design: Meinhard von Gerkan with Magdalene Weiss.
Partner: Nikolaus Goetze. **Gross floor area:**
20,000 m².

The colour of the sky

ARCHITECTS: gmp – Architekten von Gerkan,
Marg und Partner

The opening in 2006 of the new deep sea port at Yang-shan, south of Shanghai, brought rapid development of traffic infrastructure, free port zones, heavy industry zones and logistics centres to the new city of Lingang. With its coloured façade, the new High Tech Park hopes to symbolise the development potential of Lingang's heavy industry zone. The simplest building method in China was chosen – concrete skeleton covered with masonry and plaster. An ostentatious large-format paint coat in white and deep blue was added as a design feature. Large-format coloured surfaces produce a sense of depth, distance, proximity as well as strong structural contrasts. Blue and anthracite horizontal bands on white surfaces create contrasts and clear graphic lines that in turn create a sense of perspective on the long factory façades. Where it appears in architecture, blue is an explicitly unnatural colour. It is not a material colour, but rather a deliberate effect. Blue relates to the colour of the sky. In Lingang this is often a hazy grey, but under favourable wind conditions a radiant blue emerges, streaked with white clouds and wisps of vapour floating in from the sea.

02

04

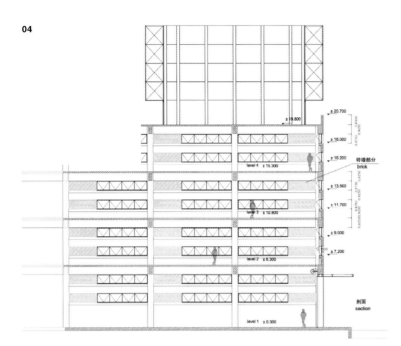

01 Colour scheme **02** Horizontal bands in white and deep blue **03** Grey ribbon windows create a sense of rhythm **04** Façade concept, tower **05** Master plan **06** Vertical gradation creates a sense of structure

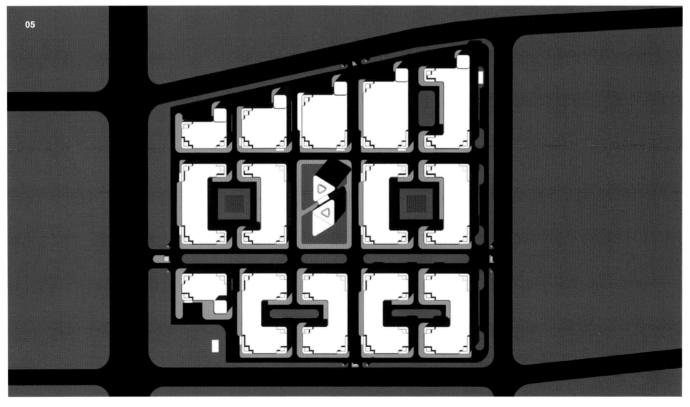

05

IT faculty building at the Technical University of Dresden, 2006
Address: Nöthnitzer Straße 60, 01187 Dresden, Germany. **Client:** Federal State of Saxony, represented by the Saxony Public Property and Building Authority, Dresden II offices. **Gross floor area:** 18,082 m².

Intense green

ARCHITECTS: Architektengemeinschaft Zimmermann * CODE UNIQUE Architekten

The materials used in the outer cladding – such as concrete, fibre cement, aluminium and glass – are also found in the interior, thereby accentuating the homogeneity of this meandering structure. However, surfaces are given different textures or material properties in different sections of the building depending on their application. The reduced colour palette is a theme that continues throughout the building – an intense shade of green on walls, floors and added elements contrasts starkly with neutral black or grey surfaces. Colour plays a central role in the design concept – it acts as an aid to orientation, strengthens the sculptural effect of certain elements and reveals the materiality of different surfaces.

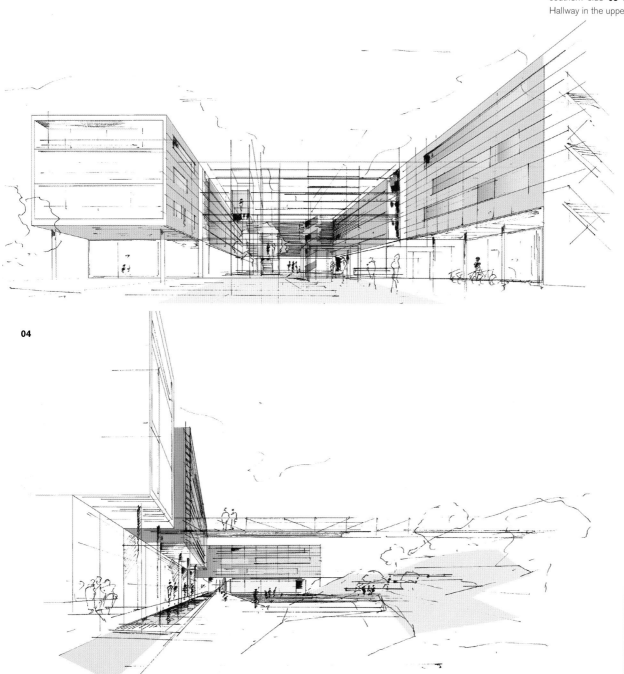

03

04

COLOURED

MUSAC in León, 2004
Address: Avenida de los Reyes Leoneses, León, Spain.
Client: Gesturcal S.A., Junta de Castilla y León. **Gross floor area:** 10,000 m².

Set of chessboards
ARCHITECTS: MANSILLA+TUÑÓN

MUSAC is a new space for culture that is widely regarded as visualising the connection between man and nature. This is a living space that opens its doors to the wide-ranging manifestations of contemporary art, an art centre that constructs a set of chessboards in which the action is determined by the protagonist of the space; a structure that develops from an open system, formed by a fabric of squares and rhombi, and permitting the construction of a secret geography of memory. Outside, the public space is a concave form that supports activities and encounters, embraced by an expanse of coloured glass in homage to the city as the place for interpersonal relationships. Inside, a large area of continuously connected, different spaces, spattered with courtyards and large skylights, shapes an expressive system that speaks to us of the interests shared by architecture and art. Five hundred prefab beams enclose a series of spaces that feature systematic repetition and formal expressiveness. MUSAC was awarded the 2007 Mies van der Rohe Prize for European Architecture.

01

04

05

Ensemble Pinnasberg, St. Pauli, 2004
Two office buildings
Address: Am Pinnasberg 45–47, 20359 Hamburg-
St. Pauli, Germany. **Gross floor area:** P45: approx.
2,000 m²; P47: approx. 4,300 m².

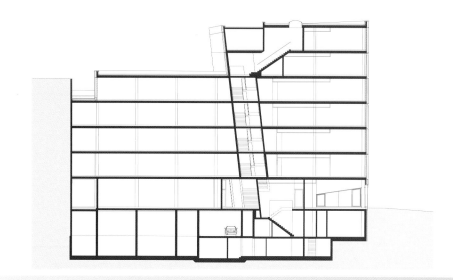

Red and green

ARCHITECTS: Spengler · Wiescholek
Architekten Stadtplaner

On a property near the harbour, in what had been waste-
land on the edge of St. Pauli, Hamburg's red light district, two vividly coloured office buildings have been built
at harbour's edge – one red, the other green. The main
building to the north is an unconventional freestanding
structure; the building to the south is decked out in a
restrained green. The red one, with its oblique façade,
commands the most attention and has been the subject
of occasional controversy. The square created to the
east of the new development offers the older buildings
in the vicinity a buffer against street noise and provides
an urban oasis at the edge of the red light district. The
southern portion has other surprises in store. Its surface is adorned with stylized ivy on enamelled glass. The
reciprocal reflection between this surface and its red
neighbour evokes a sensation of lightness.

02

01 Dock 47, longitudinal section **02** Inner courtyard situation
03 Dock 47

Fire and police station for the government district, Berlin, 2004
Address: Alt Moabit 143–145, 10557 Berlin, Germany.
Client: City Government, Berlin. **Gross floor area:**
6,850 m². **Material new façade:** glass.

Fire brigade red – police green
ARCHITECTS: Sauerbruch Hutton, Berlin

The construction of a new building for Police Station 34 and the fire brigade that serves the government district will add to a freestanding, 19th-century edifice. A side-wing of this representative old building, in which all of the rooms are located to one side of a corridor, is being used to open up a new section of the building, a suspended glass unit that will nestle against the stone firewall of the existing structure. The grounds immediately surrounding serve as a vehicle yard. Because the ensemble is situated some 20 metres from the street, facing away, and is about 6 metres lower than pavement level, pedestrian access to the old building is provided via a bridge to the first floor. The "entrance" through a window in the imposing old façade is both a pragmatic measure and a gesture emanating from the surrealism of the location. With its large glass "shingles," the façade of the new annex celebrates the formal and material contrast between an urban fragment of Berlin and its new extension. The colours used – red and green – both allude to the identifying colours of the building's two occupants and play on the contrast of colour between the existing masonry structure and the dense clusters of trees that surround it.

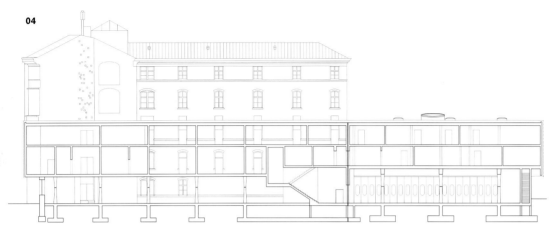

04

01 Glass façade with large-scale shingles **02** Covered parking underneath the floating annex **03** Fire brigade **04** Section cc **05** Ground floor **06** The new two-storey slab "hugs" the existing building

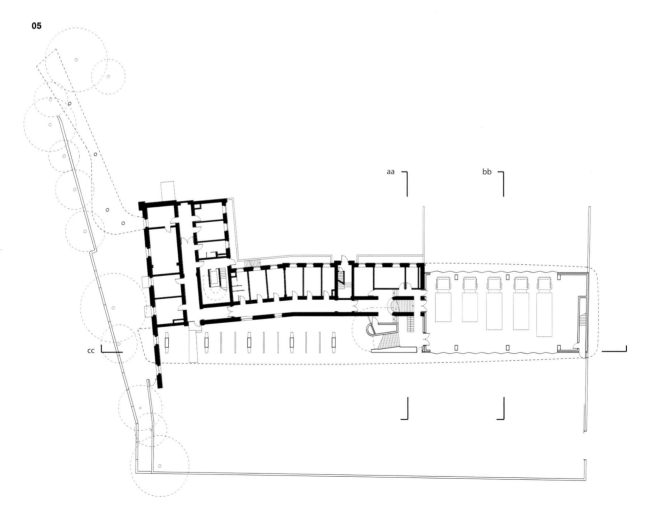

05

aa   bb

cc

Occupational Rehabilitation Centre Oberhausen, 2007
Training and dormitory building with administrative offices, conference area, and canteen with full kitchen, for about 1,000 persons
Address: Bebelstrasse 56, 46049 Oberhausen, Germany. **Lighting design for the canteen:** Ulrike Brandi Licht. **Refectory wall:** Anke Hess, Cologne. **Client:** Nordrhein-Westfälisches Berufsförderungswerk e.V. **Gross floor area:** approx. 79,000 m². **Materials:** existing: concrete; redevelopment: aluminium-glass façades (F 30), for which sheet metal shelves have been constructed with colourful sheet metal shells (F 90); expansion as dry construction.

Homage to the 1970s
ARCHITECTS: Pook Leiska Partner
Dipl. Ing. Architekten

Since 1978 the occupational rehabilitation centre in Oberhausen has offered a place of training and rehabilitation for over 1,000 people. The high-rise dormitory that dominates the complex has received a facelift in conjunction with enlargement of the rooms, turning the concrete fortress-like structure into an open and colourful building. The façade has been moved out beyond the plane formed by the front of the balconies, the concrete balustrades replaced with glass. The building's structure remains recognisable, however, as ceilings and bulkhead walls have been clad in glass panels. Marking a contrast with these are the red and green tones of closed façade bays in the form of sheet metal "boxes" of various dimensions, which curve outward and provide shelving on the inside. The entire redevelopment project and the new building on the opposite side of the street, particularly the choice of colours, represents a confrontation with the 1970s. Orange and green have been retained and reincorporated in interaction with the light grey and white tones.

04

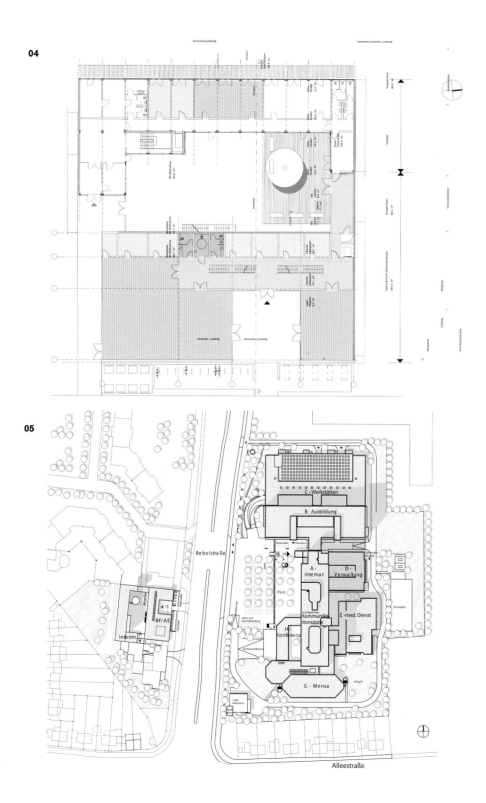

01 Western façade **02** Redeveloped hallway, dormitory (old building) **03** Façade detail **04** Ground floor plan Assessment Centre and dormitory (new building) **05** Site plan **06** Entrance area, Assessment Centre **07** Hallway, dormitory (new building)

05

Bebelstraße

Alleestraße

C - Werkstätten
B - Ausbildung
A - Internat
D - Verwaltung
E - med. Dienst
Kommunikationszone
Konferenz
G - Mensa
Interim
BF/AE

Gustav-von-Schmoller School, 2003
Address: Frankfurter Strasse 63, 74072 Heilbronn, Germany. **Client:** Municipality of Heilbronn. **Gross floor area:** 4,560 m². **Materials:** ceramic tiles (10 x 10 cm, curved surface, dark blue), Solnhofer stone, acoustic panels (Herakustik), concrete.

The old faces the new
ARCHITECTS: Lederer + Ragnarsdóttir + Oei

This school building, located close to Heilbronn central railway station, is an extension to an existing vocational school, much of which dates from the late 1950s. The ensemble is characterised by undulating forms, typical of the dynamic architecture of that period. To shield the school from noise, the façade facing the busy street is largely opaque. The problem of natural light is solved using bay windows with wavy prefab elements. In addition to the main façade a linear corridor connects the classrooms on the upper floors. Apart from the entrance foyer, the ground floor also accommodates the library and assembly hall with its curved walls. Combined with the existing school building, the L-shaped extension creates an introverted schoolyard. The old and the new entrance doors face each other. Thus, the central position of the old pavilion has been strengthened. The wavy roof of the pavilion is matched by curved walls and ground floor windows that eschew right angles.

01

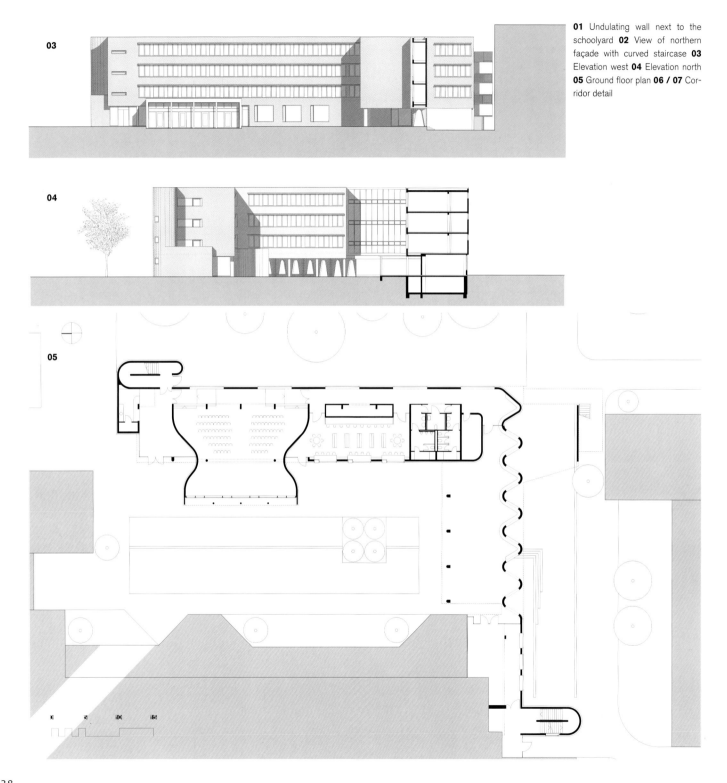

01 Undulating wall next to the schoolyard **02** View of northern façade with curved staircase **03** Elevation west **04** Elevation north **05** Ground floor plan **06 / 07** Corridor detail

03

04

05

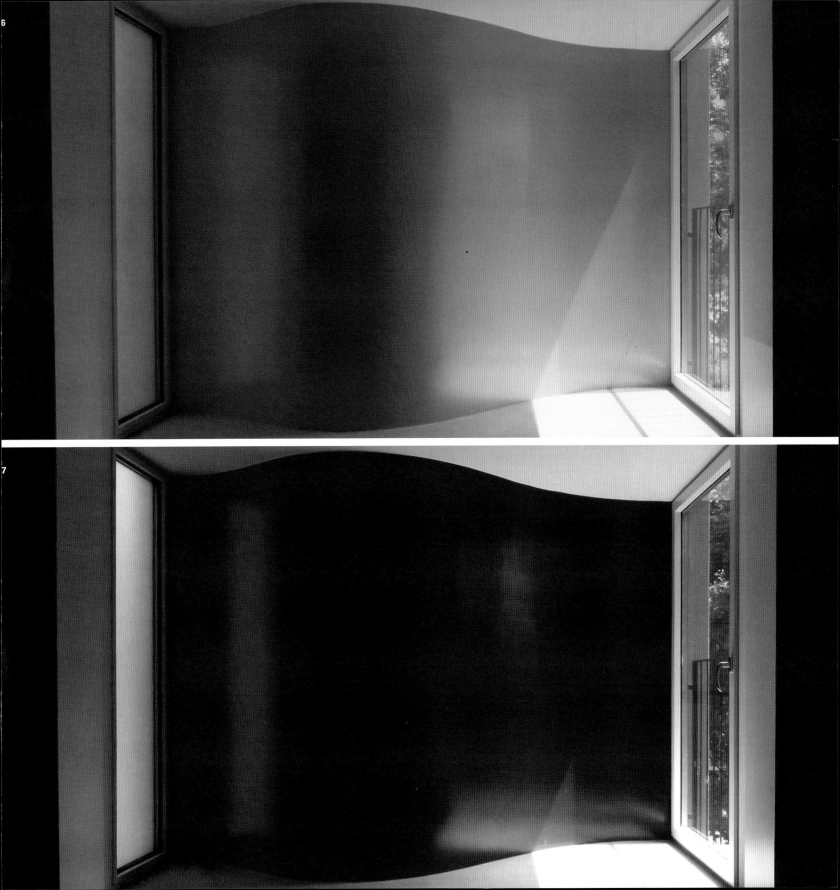

01

Centre for Marine and Atmospheric Sciences, 2003
Address: Bundesstraße 53, 20146 Hamburg, Germany.
Client: City of Hamburg Science and Research Authority and the Max Planck Society. **Gross floor area:** 9,286 m². **Materials:** façades of pigmented cast stone and printed glass panels.

Ocean-green and sky-blue
ARCHITECTS: MRLV Architekten, Hamburg
Markovic Ronai Lütjen Voss

Two new wings have been developed on a Z-shaped ground plan – one housing the Max Planck Institute for Meteorology, the other home to the University of Hamburg's Institute for Oceanography. The common entrance hall is located at the point where the two wings meet. The green roof provides a fifth façade that is visible from the neighbouring high-rise Geomatikum (geophysics building). The vertical façades are coloured oceanic-green and sky-blue, reflecting the function of the building. The recessed areas are screened by a glass membrane, and spacious atria with light directing elements guide natural light along the corridors and into the shared library and seminar areas on the ground floor.

02

04

05

06

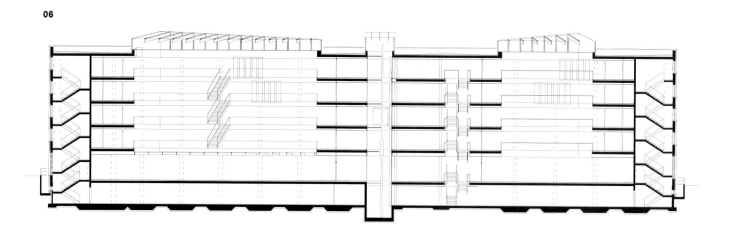

01 Exterior view **02** Internal connections **03** Atrium north **04** Ground floor plan **05** Upper floor plan **06** Longitudinal section **07** Detail glass balustrades

142

University of Applied Sciences Zittau campus, 2006
Auditorium building / institute building for the architecture and structural engineering faculties
Address: Theodor-Körner-Allee 8, 02763 Zittau, Germany. **Client:** Saxony State Authority for Property and Construction, Bautzen office. **Gross floor area:** 5,381 m². **Materials:** reinforced concrete, plaster, aluminium, epoxy resin, linoleum, cast stone.

Both refined and compelling
ARCHITECTS:

Tilman Bock Norbert Sachs Architekten

The new auditorium building at the University of Zittau, by virtue of its exposed location, forms the entrance to the new campus. "The auditorium structure reveals itself as a walk-in sculpture that offers the surprising luxury of a theatrically stepped roof terrace above the main auditorium. From there the line of sight and path of light reaches obliquely through the two-storey foyer all the way to the forecourt – a highly complex development of space that one scarcely suspects to find behind the white exterior wall surfaces," writes the critic Wolfgang Kil. Compared to the shimmering white of the auditorium building, the laboratory pavilions are a subdued grey. Colour is finally brought into play with the laboratory buildings. One of them is dominated by a green colour scale, the other by orange. The colours in each case give dominant, even garish emphasis to the stairwells and sanitary facilities. The more subdued and tasteful curtains behind the windows lend the dark plaster façades a more noble aspect.

01

02

04

05

06

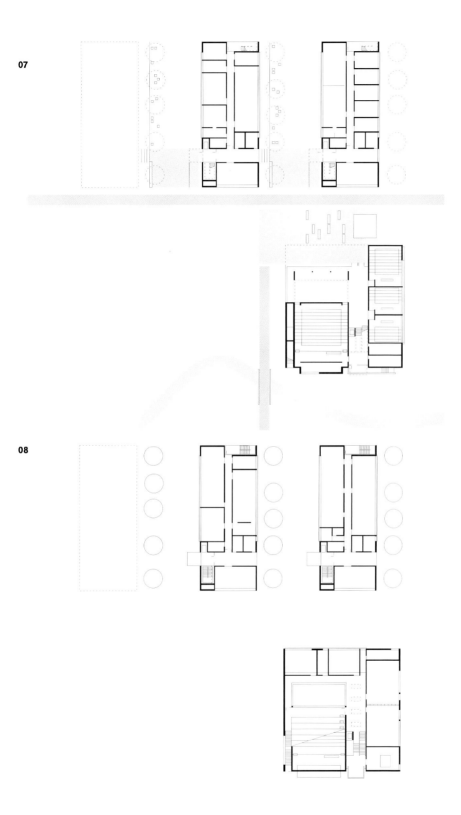

07

08

01 Roof terrace **02** View from the seminar room into the hallway **03** View from historical city ring **04** Staircase green building **05** Audimax **06** Staircase orange building **07** Ground floor plan **08** Upper floor plan

Federal Environmental Agency Dessau, 2005
Address: Federal Environmental Agency Dessau, Am Wörlitzer Platz 1, 06844 Dessau, Germany. **Client:** Federal Republic of Germany. **Gross floor area:** 40,000 m².

Complexity and simplicity combined
ARCHITECTS: Sauerbruch Hutton, Berlin

The Federal Environmental Agency's new offices are a showpiece of ecological construction, a fact reflected in the many honours and prizes it has won. "Active and passive strategies for the reduction of energy consumption and carbon dioxide production are realised in an architecture that combines spatial and material economy with a deliberate stimulation of the senses." (Sauerbruch Hutton). Though stretching to more than 250 metres in length, the offices of the Federal Environmental Agency present a remarkably consistent exterior. The dominant feature is the elegant wooden façade, which suggests sustainability rather than ecology. This is upstaged by a high-tech glass and steel structure that tumbles over the entrance area like a cascade and envelops the remaining snaking structure with a jagged sawtooth roof. The architects' careful yet exemplary use of colour in the façade defines the building's overall impact. A further feature that both influences energy use and makes a lasting visual impact is the atrium in the centre of the building. Through use of plants and water it simulates exterior space in an interior setting.

03

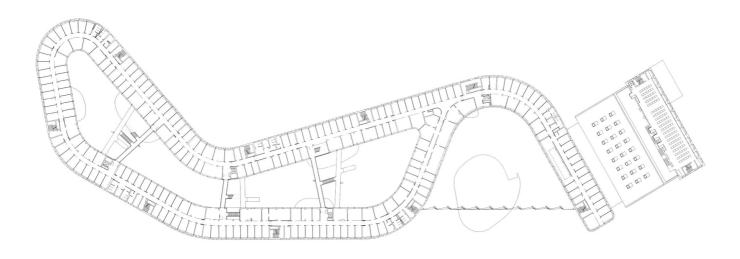

04

05

DORINT SOFITEL Bayerpost, Munich, 2004
Address: Bayerstraße 12, 80335 Munich, Germany.
Client: Dr. Herbert Ebertz & Partner GmbH. **Floor
area:** 34,600 m². **Architects:** Prof. Angerer & Hadler,
Munich. **Materials:** parquet floor, shell limestone,
leather, Indian slate, bronze mosaic and Rosso Levanto
marble form a dramaturgical arch that entices the
guest through the exciting and changeable light and
dark zones of the hotel setting.

Hotel of flowing light
INTERIOR DESIGNERS: Bert Haller,
Innenarchitekten, Mönchengladbach

The former Royal Bavarian General Post Office in Munich (built between 1896 and 1900) stood empty for
many years. Recently it has been converted to a luxury
hotel where guests experience alternate zones of shadow and light, comparable to a river flowing over rocks
and moss. The existing natural stone façades in Italian
High Renaissance style have been restored and the historic outer façade now conceals a modern core. When
one enters the building a sculpture catches the eye: a
podium clad in bronze gauze, several storeys high, is the
focus of a brilliant light show. This light sculpture creates space and dominates the airy central foyer, which
is crowned by a voluminous glass cupola. Taken together, the effect is a gala of light and colour.

01

01 Façade detail **02** Lobby **03** Ground floor plan **04** Longitudinal section **05** Wellness **06** Bed detail

03

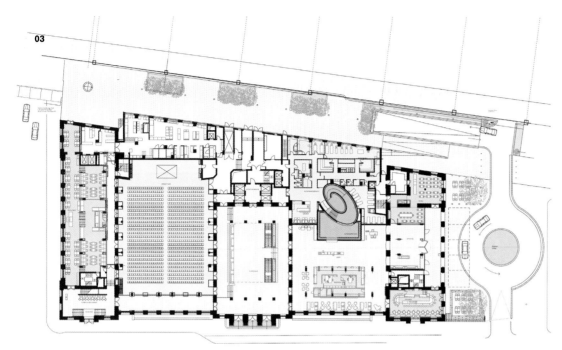

04

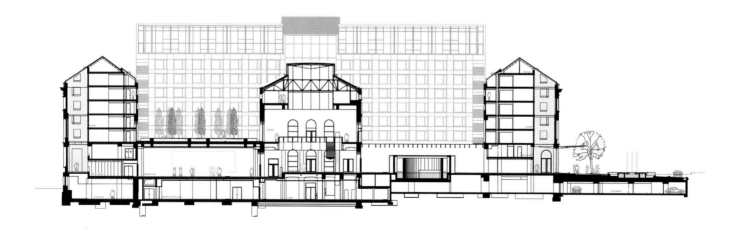

Oberstufenschule (senior-grade secondary school)
Breite, Hinwil ZH, 2004
Address: Breitestrasse 6, 8340 Hinwil, Switzerland.
Client: Hinwil senior-grade secondary school com-
munity. **Landscape architect:** Hager Landschaftsar-
chitektur AG, Zurich. **Artist:** Thomas Rutherfoord,
Winterthur. **Gross floor area:** 2,400 m². **Materials:**
Plastered single-stone masonry (insulation bricks),
windows, walls and cabinets in oak, granolithic con-
crete flooring.

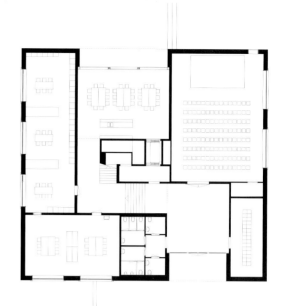

Eyes in the landscape

ARCHITECTS: Gafner & Horisberger
Architekten GmbH

The Oberstufenschule Breite buildings and grounds
were developed over three phases (1953, 1972, 2004).
A colour scheme for the entire building was developed
in close cooperation with the artist Thomas Rutherford.
The architectural idea of a solid monolithic building
manifests itself as a warm, earth-brown-coloured exterior. This somewhat dark colour scheme is given an additional injection of life by the use of glazing techniques
in the paint coating. This allows the building to assume
a variety of shades, hues and depths depending on the
time of day and the season. In contrast to the exterior
the internal walls are covered with light-coloured glass-
fibre wallpaper. Thanks to large window openings the
internal colour scheme seeps out to the exterior and
has an additional enlivening and enlightening effect on
the façade. At the same time these windows are the
eyes through which the building looks out upon the
Zurich Oberland.

01 Floor plan **02** Group room **03** View from the north west

St. Afra's boarding grammar school, Meißen, 2003
Address: Freiheit 13, 01662 Meißen, Germany. **Urban planning:** Jörg Friedrich & Partner, Hamburg. **Client:** State of Saxony represented by the State Building Authority in Dresden. **Gross floor area:** 15,000 m².

Order and chaos
ARCHITECTS (project planning):
Maedebach, Redeleit & Partner, Berlin

The individual buildings within the residential area are connected by a definite geometric contour. An apparently rigid sense of order permits great freedom in the interiors. Order and chaos, planning and spontaneity, rules and freedom. These paired concepts play a major role in the lives of young people, and here they define the educational idea behind this very special school. The buildings within the residential cluster are constructed using just a few basic elements. Each building develops its own character, a process in which colour plays an important role. All of the pupils' apartments are located off a coloured corridor wall. This "leading colour" continues on the staircase. Due to the extensive use of glass, the sense of colour permeates to the exterior in a sublime way. That is why the façades required only slight touches of colour. The architects used a palette of five different shades of white. On certain parts of the external wall – recessed plastered areas next to the windows – the leading colour once again appears in a fuller, darker tone. These scuncheons clearly reveal that the sense of colour emanates from the interior of these buildings.

158

04

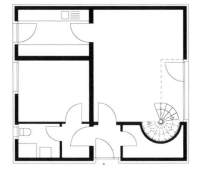 

01 Pupils' buildings **02** "Leading colours" **03** Residential cluster **04** Ground and upper floor plan mentor's house **05** Floor plan pupils' building **06** Site plan **07** Pupils' buildings

05

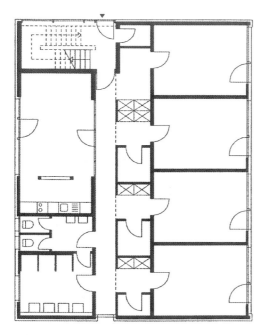

06

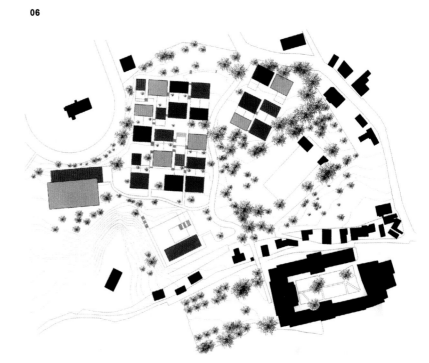

Turin Olympic Village, 2006
Address: Via Giordano Bruno, Turin, Italy. **Colour scheme:** Erich Wiesner, Berlin. **Client:** Agenzia Torino 2006. **Gross floor area:** 20,000 m². **Materials:** reinforced concrete structure with two-withe external walls, plastered.

Flying the flag
ARCHITECTS (of Site 3): Steidle Architekten, responsible partner: Johannes Ernst

The Olympic Village for the 2006 Winter Olympic Games in Turin, a city developed on a grid, explored the continuation and extension of that structure. This permitted the development of multi-purpose squares and courtyards for the community based on an ordered structure. Form, façade and colour are the defining themes of this quarter. It was inspired by the idea of a colourful forest of international flags. From there a friendly struggle developed between two colour tones that competed for dominance. While this appears very emblematic at first glance, it has mostly met with amused approval. The office of Otto Steidle, who sadly died in 2004, established an international reputation for developing people-friendly residential buildings, a factor that also emerges from a glance at the floor plans for this project.

04

EDIFICIO B0 (CASA 1)

EDIFICIO D0 (CASA 2)

EDIFICIO F0 (CASA 3)

EDIFICIO C1 (CASA 6)

EDIFICIO B2 (CASA 7)

EDIFICIO D2 (CASA 8)

EDIFICIO F2 (CASA 9)

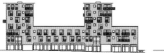

EDIFICIO A4 - C4 (CASA 10 r11)

164

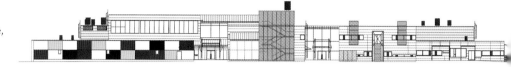

Mikkola School, 2005
Address: Vantaa, Finland. **Client:** City of Vantaa.
Gross floor area: 5,950 m². **Materials:** steel structure, steel plate façades.

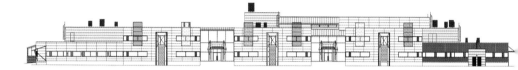

Key role
ARCHITECTS: Esa Piironen Architects

The new extension is built on a tree-covered slope at the northwest end of Mikkola Comprehensive School, which was originally constructed in 1974. The external surfaces are light in colour, but the various parts have been enhanced with bright colours. The principle materials used in the façade include white steel sheet panels, light grey steel sheeting for air conditioning ducts and technical workshop walls, and light-coloured steel mesh walls on the external staircases, painted on the inside in a variety of colours. The external walls are built of prefabricated thermal profile elements. The plinths and the external surface of the civic shelter are made of prefabricated reinforced concrete elements. Colour plays a key role in this school. First of all, white makes the space very light, which is especially important in this northern climate. Bright primary colours on exterior details gives the building a friendly appearance. The colourful façade at the main entrance also has a welcoming and enticing effect.

01 Elevations north west and south west **02** Main entrance **03** Main lobby with view into gymnasium

Rehabilitation of St. Caterina Market, Barcelona, 2005
Address: Avinguda Francesc Cambó s/n, Barcelona, Spain. **Client:** Foment de Ciutat Vella S.A. **Engineer (Roof):** Jose Maria Velasco. **Materials:** steel and wooden framework; laminated wooden roof; hexagonal ceramic tiles.

The fifth façade
ARCHITECTS:
Enric Miralles Benedetta Tagliabue
Miralles Tagliabue – EMBT, Barcelona

The power of this experiment lies in the fith façade, the roof. A colourful, undulating carpet of ceramic is laid over old walls and a modern supporting structure. Seen from above the patchwork of colours reminds one of what is on sale here – colourful fruit and vegetables. Viewed from the street the dominant forms are the rippling vaults of the roof edges. Here EMBT's touch is light and energetic, a brilliant icon for selling the colourful life of Barcelona. The roof panels were made of laminated wood that had to be hand-cut in sections to fit the awkward curves. For all its computer-generated sophistication, the roof is largely hand-crafted. The surface is finished in hexagonal ceramic tiles that were specially made in Seville and were designed to evoke the produce below.

05

01 Detail 02 The roof viewed from the new housing blocks 03 The ceramic roof 04 New public piazza 05 Ground plan and section 06 Ceramic roof plan 07 Interior view over the market 08 Principal entrance and roof perspective

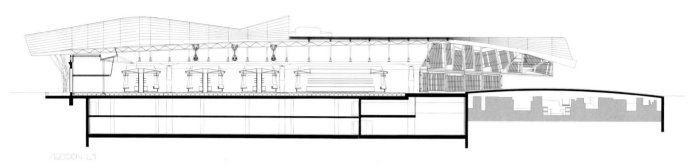

SECCIÓN L1

06

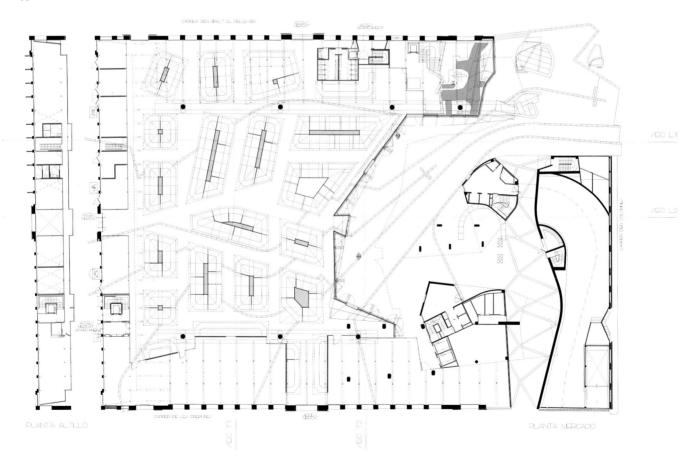

PLANTA ALTILLO

PLANTA MERCADO

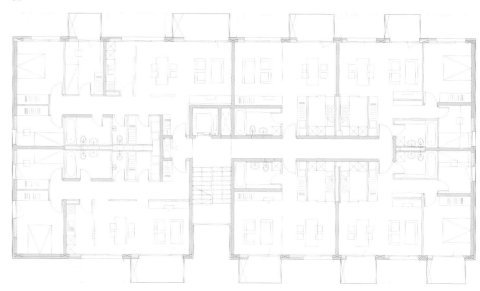

Social housing on the coast, 2005
Address: Livade, Izola, Slovenia. **Gross floor area:**
5,452 m². **Materials:** concrete construction grid with
brick fillings, plaster, precast laminates.

Beehive
ARCHITECTS: OFIS arhitekti

This project is a winning entry for two housing blocks in a competition run by the Slovenian Housing Fund, a government-run programme that provides low-cost housing for young families. This proposal won for a mixture economic, rational and functional reasons, but mostly for the ratio between gross and saleable surface area and the flexibility of the plans. The blocks are set out on a hill with a view of Izola Bay on one side and of the surrounding hills on the other. Since the buildings are located in a Mediterranean climate, outdoor space and shade are important elements. The project proposed a veranda for each apartment, thus providing an outdoor space that is intimate, partly connected with the interior, shady and naturally ventilated. The idea of the coloured balconies was based on existing ones in Izola that have been redesigned by residents in a variety of ways and using a variety of colours. The architects wanted to produce the same atmosphere by combining coloured balconies and awnings. The result reminded people of a honey-comb structure or beehive.

01 Level 1 **02** Social housing **03** Social housing

Eternit Headquarters, Heidelberg, 2007
Offices, conference rooms, showroom
Address: Im Breitspiel 20, 69126 Heidelberg, Germany.
Design: Astrid Bornheim, Berlin. **Façade:** in coopera-
tion with DKO Architects, Berlin. **Interiors:** construc-
tion management Peter von Klitzing. **Art design:**
Astrid Bornheim with Folke Hanfeld, Berlin.
Client: Eternit AG. **Materials:** fibre cement, glass,
metal.

01

Laboratory of ideas
ARCHITECTS: Astrid Bornheim, Berlin

The dominant colour of the showroom is the same as
Eternit material: cement grey. The colour scheme in this
room is borrowed from the company logo: Against the
background of a white, jointless epoxy resin floor and
the grey passe-partout of fibre cement furniture the red
and green logo colours appear on glasses, chairs and
dishes. The bar counter is clad with fibre cement and
tiled with green glass. The wash basin, a sloping green
pane of glass, runs off into a stainless steel channel. The
fibre cement material is thus protected from moisture
and yet forms the stabile, character-forming body of the
washing area. The chairs in the training room produce
a kind of shadow play with white moulded seats and
green or red backs. The lighting, by its very lightness,
is also in keeping with the rational-technical ideas of
the distinguished German architect Ernst Neufert. Here
the designers also opted for a novel product: a delicate
glass bar that can act both as a cold, white fluorescent
light and a dimmable halogen spotlight.

02

04

01 Red green wave on east façade
02 / 03 Red green code on fibre
cement gable **04** Showroom concept: moveable boxes **05** Ground-
floor: colour and surface concept
06 Empty showcases **07** Solid fibre cement furniture vs. bright light
structure

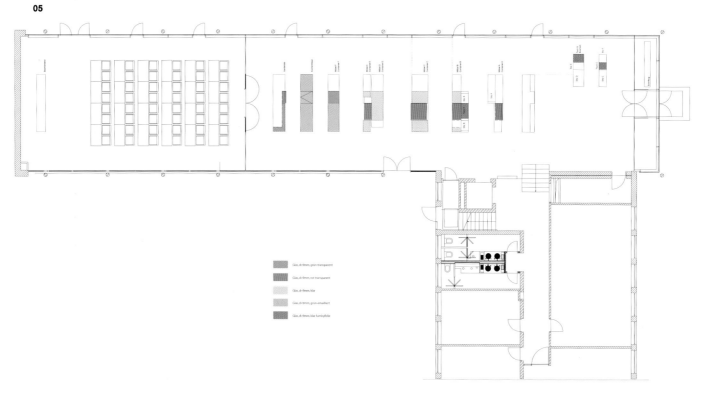

01 ARCHITEKTENORDNER
   PRODUKTINFORMATIONEN

02 DACH- UND
   FASSADENPLATTEN

03 FASSADE GROSSFORMAT

04 HOLZ- UND
   AUSBAU

05 WELLPLATTEN
   DACHSTEINE

06 DACH- UND
   FASSADENPLATTEN

06

05

04

03

02

01

05

Glas, d=9mm, grün transparent

Glas, d=9mm, rot transparent

Glas, d=9mm, klar

Glas, d=9mm, grün-emailliert

Glas, d=9mm, klar-furnisyfolie

Hotel Puerta America, Madrid, 2005
Address: Avenida de América. 41, 28002 Madrid,
Spain. **Local architect:** Alberto Medem TEMA – Taller
Estudio Medem Arquitectos. S.L. **Client:** Groupe
URVASCO Cadena Hotelera SILKEN. **Gross floor
area:** 12th floor: 1,336 m², 13th floor: 1,320 m².

Playground of ideas
ARCHITECTS: Ateliers Jean Nouvel

Almost 20 international architects were involved in designing this hotel. Jean Nouvel contributed the façade,
the 12th floor with suites and the 13th floor with swimming pool and panoramic bar. His façade looks like an
elegant paint box and makes this building simply impos-
sible to ignore. It announces to all that a similarly colourful kaleidoscope of architectural postures and interior
design signatures can be expected within – designed
by luminaries such as Norman Foster, Ron Arad, Ushida
Findlay or Zaha Hadid. The 12th floor is impressive not
only for its magnificent views, but also for its trick box of
virtual and real effects in colour and glass. With around
350 rooms the Puerta America is among the world's
largest design hotels – and undoubtedly the largest
playground of hotel architecture anywhere.

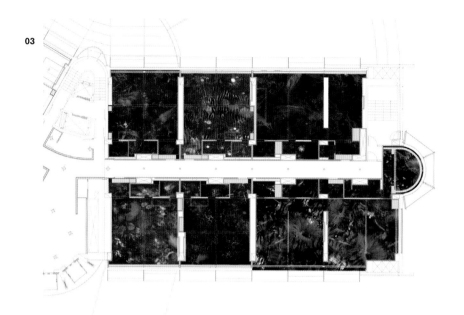

03

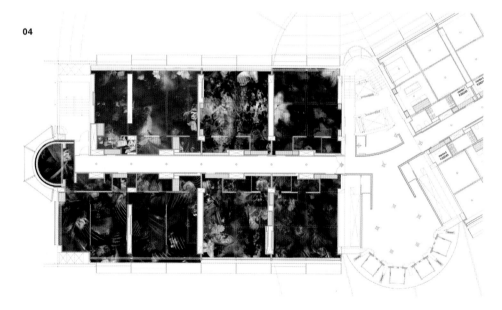

04

05

01 Bathroom in the suite with photos by Roland Fleischer on the walls and ceiling **02** Suite with photos by Roland Fleischer on the walls and ceiling **03** Floor plan with ceiling image by Roland Fleischer **04** Floor plan with ceiling image by Nobuyoshi Araki **05** Longitudinal section 13th floor: swimming pool and bar **06** Suite behind a photo by Nobuyoshi Araki

Revival of historic Clarke Quay, Singapore, 2005
Materials: street roofs: ETFE foil cushions supported by steelwork structures.

Happy shopping
ARCHITECTS: SMC ALSOP, London

The diamond-shaped site has along its waterfront a series of traditional shops with well proportioned, colonnaded five-foot walkways behind. The architects were faced with three principle tasks: first, to revive the riverfront with a series of raised "lily pad" dining platforms and "bluebell" membrane canopies to enliven the waterfront area; second, to produce shade over the streets that dissect the site. The intention here is to mitigate the extremes of Singapore's climate. The "environmental angels" act as chimney vents, providing shade and ventilation at ground level by both passive and active means. The third intervention is a new urban entertainment block along River Valley Road moving away from the river. This creates a new, dynamic and stronger presence for Clarke Quay from River Valley Road, and from Fort Canning beyond.

01 Aerial view **02** Environmental angels **03** Bluebell canopies

01

Dalki Theme Park, 2006
Address: H-69-1 Heyri Art Valley, KyungGi, South Korea. **Client:** Ssamzie Corporation. **Gross floor area:** 2,453.51 m².

Real virtuality

ARCHITECTS: Ga.A architects + Yonsei University (Moongyu Choi) / Mass Studies (Minsuk Cho) / Slade Architecture (James Slade)

Dalki is a cartoon character that was created to market clothes and other products for children and teenagers. She is an imaginary girl who lives in a garden with her friends. Dalki Theme Park is a building where these imaginary characters interact with human visitors in a real, physical setting. The space accommodates shopping, playing, eating and lounging as well as exhibits dealing with scale, nature and the Dalki characters. The building encompasses three vertical zones. The open ground level is a scaleless artificial garden. Different program areas spread throughout the raised interior space encourage free movement between programs. A garden and lounge on the roof extend the natural landscape, establishing a point of reference to the lush surrounding landscape. Rather than abstracting from nature, the building is a synthetic hyper-representation of nature (meta-real): mimicking while questioning the nature of nature. Merging these levels into each other and into the site creates a seamless transition between zones and between building and site.

02

07

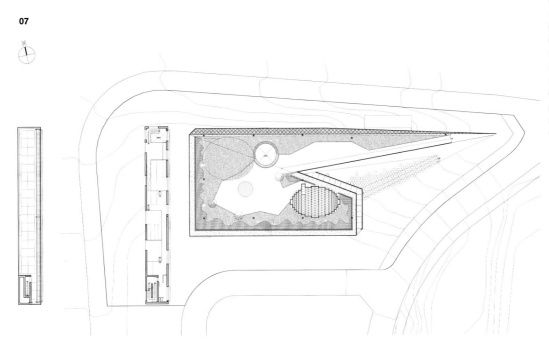

01 Sod roof and walls 02 Grassy rooftop garden of Dalki theme park 03 Two entrances from the terrace 04 Spiral staircase connecting the second floor to the exhibition space on the first floor 05 Lounge space with built-in wood seating 06 Artificial terrace garden on the ground level 07 Roof plan of the site 08 Longitudinal sections of the site

08

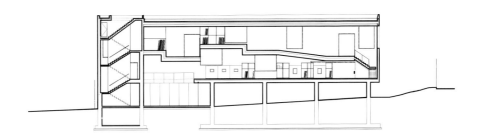

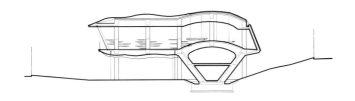

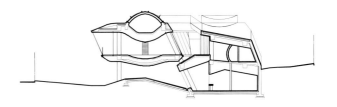

Bodies, 2006
Women's-only fitness studio
Address: various major cities across Japan. **Client:**
Bodies Co. Ltd.. **Gross floor area:** 144.80 m²
(Kameari studio). **Materials:** Floors: tile carpeting,
vinyl flooring; Walls: white and beige acrylic enamel
paint; Ceiling: white acrylic enamel paint.

Three-dimensional
ARCHITECTS: Emmanuelle Moureaux

Bodies is a women's-only fitness studio located in various major cities in Japan – in department stores, shopping centres and railway stations. The client wanted to create a new brand image by designing everything from the interior design to the graphics. The concept: yellow, pink, and green colours in addition to the Bodies' original brand colour orange. Inspired by traditional Japanese textile screens – "Noren" and "Kabeshiro" – the colourful partition series Emmanuelle called "Shikiri" was adopted in this project. Colour plays an important role in this project as a means of dividing space. The gradation of colours moving in circles symbolizes a circuit workout environment. Colours appear in three-dimensional form (coloured felt screens divide the space). Emmanuelle worked to bring out the best in each space by carefully selecting the most suitable vibrant colours to create a memorable image of the space and provide a highly tactile experience for people within the space.

04

05

06

07

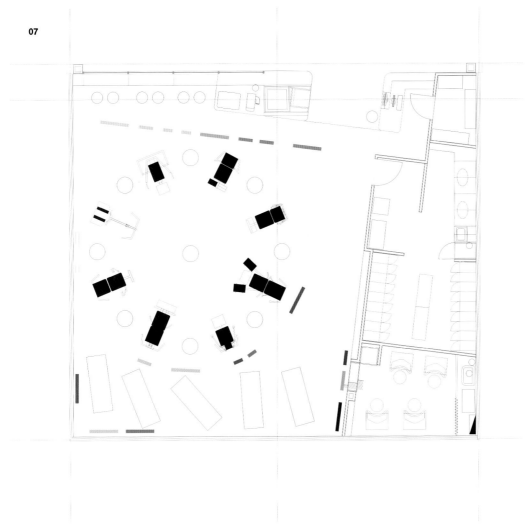

01 Circuit area and equipments **02** Circuit area and Shikiri Felt Partition **03** Entrance **04** Shikiri Felt Partition – close up shot **05** Entrance **06** Circuit area in shimmer light **07** Bodies plan **08** Bodies elevation

08

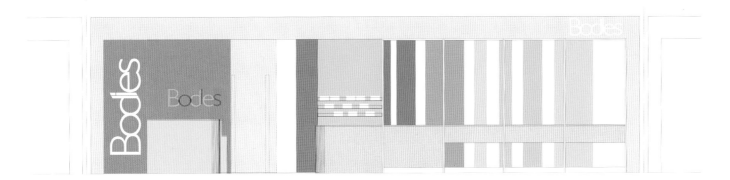

Cabaret Voltaire – Dada Zurich, 2004
Address: Spiegelgasse 1, 8001 Zurich, Switzerland.
Client: Präsidialdepartement of the City of Zurich.
Gross floor area: 325 m². **Materials:** pigmented, sanded fibre cement panels, Eternit Pelicolor Carat, various colours (charcoal grey, ruby, amber).

Birth of Dada
ARCHITECTS: Rossetti + Wyss
Architekten AG, Zurich

The Dada House at Spiegelgasse 1 is no ordinary building. Here, in the birthplace of Dadaism, architects regard it as a dynamic, contemporary cultural site. The structural alterations needed to incorporate the cabaret have been reduced to functional elements, thus maintaining the Dada focus in the four main rooms. The design pays special attention to the passages between rooms, implanting the needed infrastructures into the old structural fabric of the building. A colour has been assigned to each of the passages. Visitors entering them find themselves immersed in a tunnel of colour. The colour is not painted on; rather, pigmented fibre cement panels are affixed to the floors, walls and ceiling. The older the structure becomes, the more intensive the colour's effect as wear and abrasion continue to give it new depth.

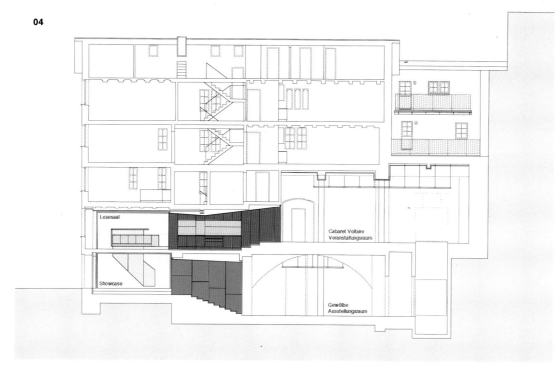

01 Detail bar **02** Detail staircase
03 Reading room with coffee bar
and library **04** Longitudinal section
05 Upper floor plan **06** Cabaret
Voltaire

Lesesaal

Showcase

Cabaret Voltaire
Veranstaltungsraum

Gewölbe
Ausstellungsraum

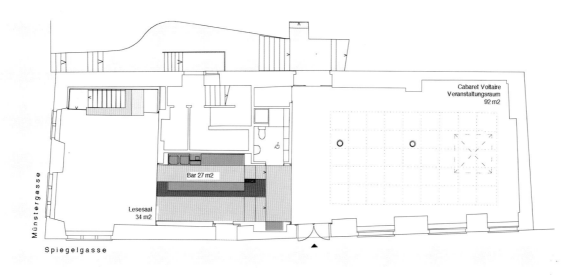

Cabaret Voltaire
Veranstaltungsraum
92 m2

Bar 27 m2

Lesesaal
34 m2

Münstergasse

Spiegelgasse

01

Sharp Centre for Design, Ontario College of Art & Design, 2004
Address: 100 McCaul Street, Toronto, Canada. **Client:** Ontario College of Art & Design. **Building expansion:** 6,215 m².

Standing tall
ARCHITECTS:
Robbie/Young + Wright Architects Inc. and Alsop Architects Ltd (Joint Venture)

The remarkable "table top" superstructure, which takes the form of a parallelepiped (9m high, 31m wide and 84m long), with striking black and white pixilated skin, stands 26 metres above the ground on 12 multi-coloured legs. This "bigfoot" structure towers over the old college building and houses two storeys of studio and teaching space. It is connected to the existing facility below by an elevator and stairwell that forms the central focus of the newly created entrance hall which unites the two halves of the existing college buildings at all levels. This new space comprises a new four-storey Entrance Hall, which is entered through a full height glass façade, and a three-storey Great Hall on Level 2, where students and artists can exhibit their work. This will be an important centre for social activity and a valuable space for events, with a gallery, auditorium, café and conference centre immediately adjacent.

02

04

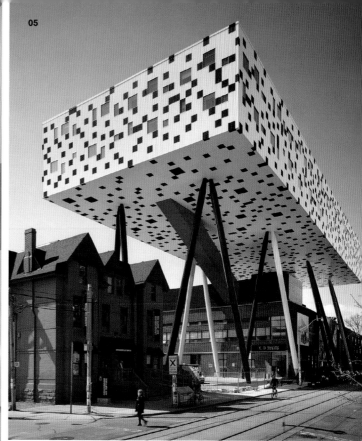

05

06

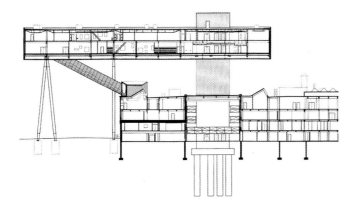

07

08

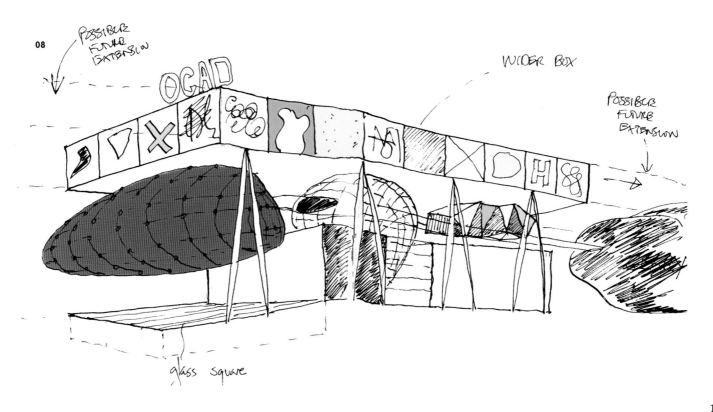

POSSIBLE FUTURE EXTENSION

OCAD

WIDER BOX

POSSIBLE FUTURE EXTENSION

glass square

Offices "La Defense", Almere, 2004
Address: "La Defense", Almere business centre, The Netherlands. **Gross floor area:** 23,000 m² offices; 15,000 m² parking.

Changing façades
ARCHITECTS: Ben van Berkel / UNStudio

This office building "La Defense" is interrupted at two points, creating a link with the park to the rear. Raising the ground level from the town side strengthened the link. Parking facilities are provided under the building rather than between the units, creating a pleasant inner area. The units vary in height from five or six to three or four levels, the top level often being doubled. As a whole the building is modest in volume and fits well within its urban surroundings which are reflected in its metallic façade. The outer skin expresses urbanity and a degree of closeness of the units. Entering the inner courtyard the building reveals its true character. The façade adjacent to the courtyard is constructed of glass panels in which a multi-coloured foil is integrated. Depending on the time of the day and the angle of incidence, the façade changes from yellow to blue, to red or from purple to green and back again.

03

04

01 / 02 View inner courtyard **03** Floor plan parking garage **04** Floor plan level 4 **05** View inner courtyard

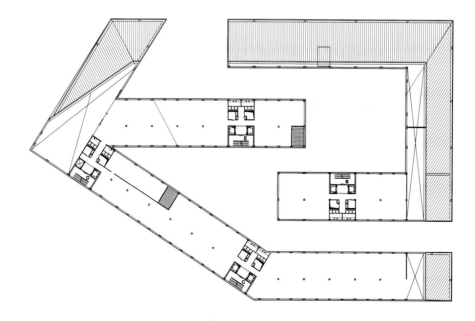

LIGHT

Torre Agbar, 2005
Address: 211 Avenida Diagonal, Barcelona, Spain.
Gross floor area: 47,500 m².

Small skyscraper

ARCHITECTS: Ateliers Jean Nouvel +
Fermín Vázquez / b720 Arquitectos

The Agbar tower is a 35-storey and 142-metre-high "small skyscraper" located in Plaza de las Glorias in Barcelona. The shape of the building emulates a fountain with constant and perfectly stable pressure. This is a very suitable image for the headquarters of a water company, reinforced by the impression that the building does not rest on the ground but rather emerges from a water-filled crater. It is constructed by means of two oval concrete cylinders which support a system of metal beams. The façade consists of corrugated aluminium sheeting lacquered in 25 colours. This cladding protects a layer of rock wool fixed to the exterior face of the wall and provides the shaft of the building with a backing that gradually changes colour. It begins at the base with reddish shades, earthy like the ground they emerge from and ends in the upper floors with blue shades that blend with the sky in an illusion of dematerialisation. The entire building is wrapped in a vibrant second skin of laminated glass slats with different degrees of transparency, thus blurring the coloured façade behind.

01 Panorama view **02** Tipo **03** External view

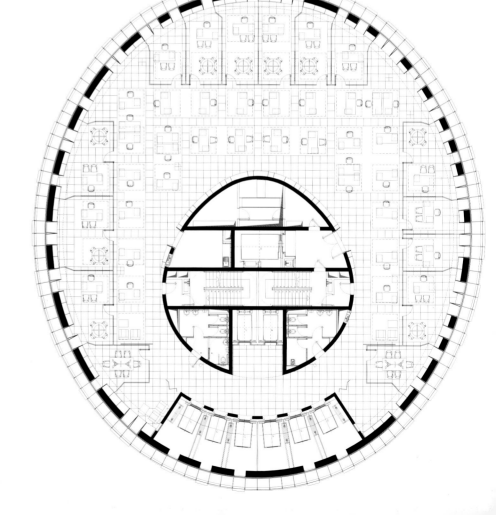

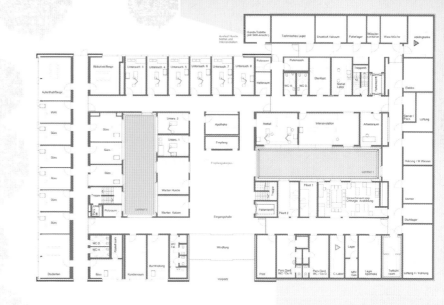

Clinic for small animals and diagnostic imaging, 2005
Address: Vetsuisse Faculty of the University of Berne, Länggassstrasse 128, 3012 Berne, Switzerland. **Planning consultants:** Reto Boller, artist, Zurich; Dr. Max Lüscher, colour psychologist, Lucerne. **Client:** AGG, Municipal Property and Buildings Authority. **Gross floor area:** 4,050 m². **Materials:** façade: non-bearing pigmented cement slabs, inner courtyards: painted mineral plaster.

The best treatment for pets
ARCHITECTS: Schär Architekten AG, Bern

A self-explanatory building that conforms with its urban business milieu while improving it at the same time. Designed as an entry for a competition whose stated objective was "to build and design spaces that go beyond the inherent order of functional clinic construction to create a distinctive and pleasant mood" (architectural commentary), it has pursued and achieved this objective to the letter. Though the unadorned room surfaces may appear restrained, they do lend the rooms a special touch. The intensive colours of the inner courtyards indirectly colour the interior, creating a variegated succession of moods that shifts with the changes in daylight.

01 Ground floor **02** Play of light in the hallway **03** Yellow courtyard
04 Entrance hall with view into the blue courtyard

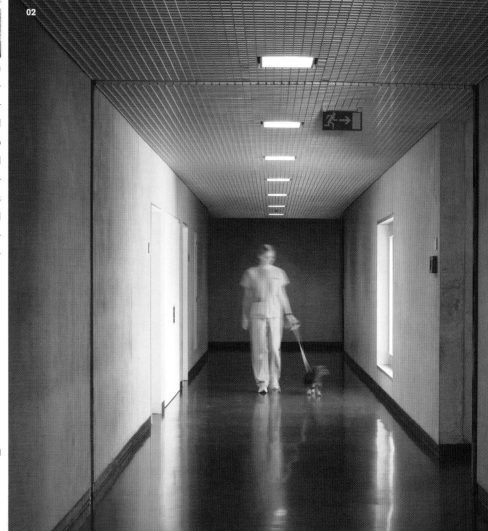

Winnenden Special School (Förderschule), 2006
Address: Albertviller Str. 36, 71364 Winnenden, Germany. **Colour scheme:** Herbert Kopp, Munich; Adler & Olesch Landscape Architects, Stuttgart. **Client:** Municipality of Winnenden. **Gross floor area:** 4,683 m². **Materials:** façade in concrete and composite thermal insulation; rubber flooring; ceiling in acoustic panels.

A school with a view
ARCHITECTS: Diezinger & Kramer
Dipl. Inge Architekten BDA

The layout of the building complex matches the educational requirements of three separate age cohorts, each of which is "housed" in a separate part of the building. Thanks to a systematic use of colour this building asserts itself optically within an otherwise "anonymous" environment. Likewise in the interior a varied use of colour creates different identities and zones. The open-space areas play an important part in the educational function of this institution. The paved forecourt provides a suitable point of entry to the school while the break and maintenance yards at the southwest end are linked together and surrounded by a protective hedge. Unusually for a school building, there is a roof garden on the second floor offering a separate rest area.

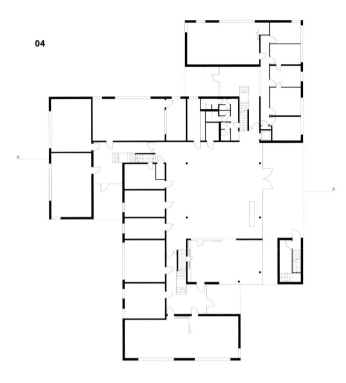

04

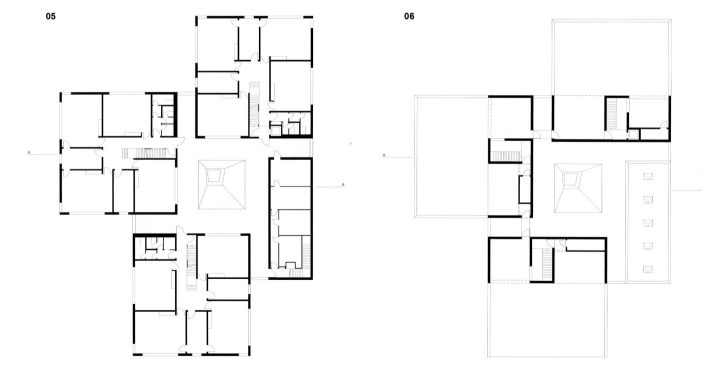

05

06

Holmes Place Lifestyle Club in Cologne, 2006
Address: Cologne Mediapark, Germany. **Client:** Holmes Place Health and Wellness AG Berlin. **Gross floor area:** 4,000 m². **Materials:** reinforced concrete skeleton, interior finish in glass, coloured polycarbonate panels, plastics, quarry stone, palisander veneer, textiles.

The colour white
ARCHITECTS: SEHW Berlin Hamburg Wien

The Holmes Place Health Club in Cologne is located on the fringe of the inner city and is part of the "Mediapark", a new commercial district. The club fills a five-storey curved structure. Due to the way the various functions are distributed over the five floors of the building, its use is apparent from the outside. One enters the club through a public square, arriving first in a spacious foyer on the ground floor. Coloured polycarbonate panels are used here as wall screens and evoke the principle form of activity in this district. Media also play a role in the furnishings of the reception area. The further one penetrates the interior of the club, the simpler and calmer its ambience becomes. The colour white is dominant here.

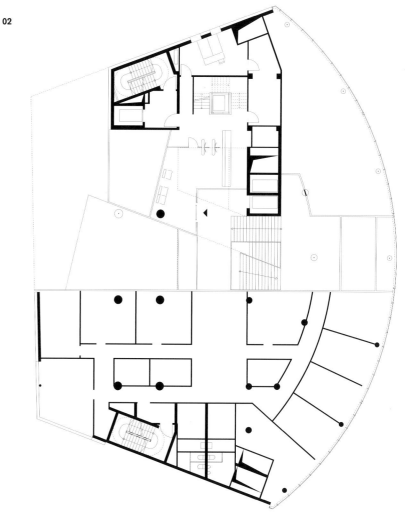

02

01 Foyer **02** Floor plan **03** Pool Relax

Netherlands Institute for Sound and Vision, 2007
Address: Sumatralaan 45, Mediapark, Hilversum,
Netherlands. **Client:** Netherlands Institute for Sound
and Vision, Hilversum. **Gross floor area:** 30,000 m².
Façade design: Neutelings Riedijk Architects in
cooperation with Bureau Bouwkunde Rotterdam.
Graphic design, façade: Jaap Drupsteen. **Development of glass panels:** Neutelings Riedijk Architects in
cooperation with T.N.O. Eindhoven, Studio Drupsteen
and Saint Gobain.

Screen and canyon
ARCHITECTS: Neutelings Riedijk Architects,
Rotterdam

The building that houses the archives of the Netherlands Institute for Sound and Vision is a blend of two
allegories: a colourful "screen" as a high-tech glass
enclosure and, underground, a safe for treasures from
the analogue era of Dutch television and radio broadcasting. The enclosure is a modern trompe l'oeil that
recounts the highlights of Dutch television history on
2,244 glass panels. To achieve the desired façade reliefs, special software was developed to transfer the
selected film scenes with the use of moulds and three
colours of ink. The pigments were burned into the glass
at 800° C at the same time that the glass was melted
into the moulds. On the inside, the ground has been
excavated to accommodate five underground levels
bounded by both steep and terraced walls. Above, this
canyon assumes its alter ego as an atrium that reaches
all the way up to the glass roof.

01 Night shot of Netherlands Institute for Sound and Vision 02 Detail of ceiling decoration and glass façade 03 Central Hall with a view at the archives 04 Situation 05 The Experience, permanent exposition 06 Cinema second floor

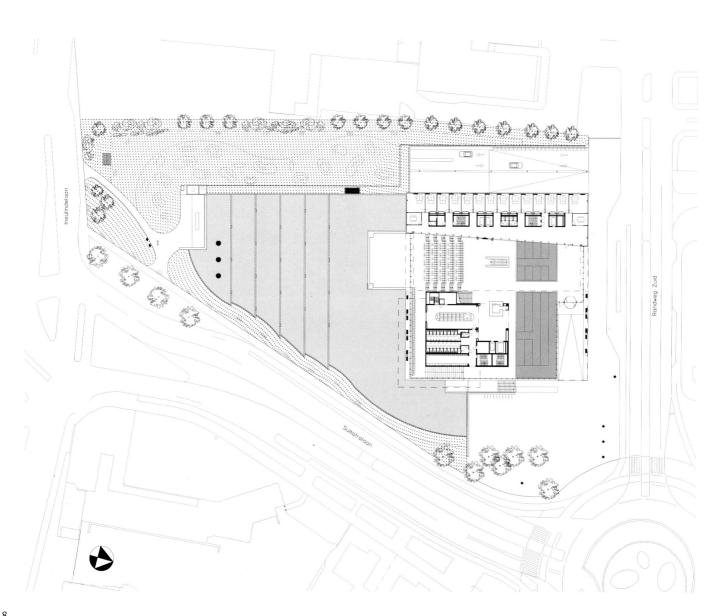

Buchfinken primary school in Usingen-Eschbach
Address: Schulstrasse 8, 61250 Usingen, Germany.
Client: Upper Taunus Rural District Authority (Land-ratsamt Hochtaununskreis). **Gross floor area:**
4,313 m². **Materials:** concrete, Eternit, steel post and rail structure, sheet zinc roofs.

An open view

ARCHITECTS: Alten Architekten, Berlin

This all-day primary school is situated at the edge of Eschbach, where it commands a magnificent view of the Taunus mountain range and the Feldberg. The individual buildings appear to gradually break away from the town-scape as they merge with the surrounding landscape. This process leads off with the red childcare building that fronts directly onto the street. This is still clearly part of the town and, in combination with the ivory-coloured, two-storey, bending wall of the adjacent building, creates a forecourt for the school. The school is entered through an expansive portal. Only a few metres beyond, through an open gallery, the view opens up again to the Feldberg to the other side.

01 Hallway 02 Upper schoolyard
03 Entrance floor 04 Section 05
Typical classroom 06 Yellow retain-
ing wall in the garden floor

03

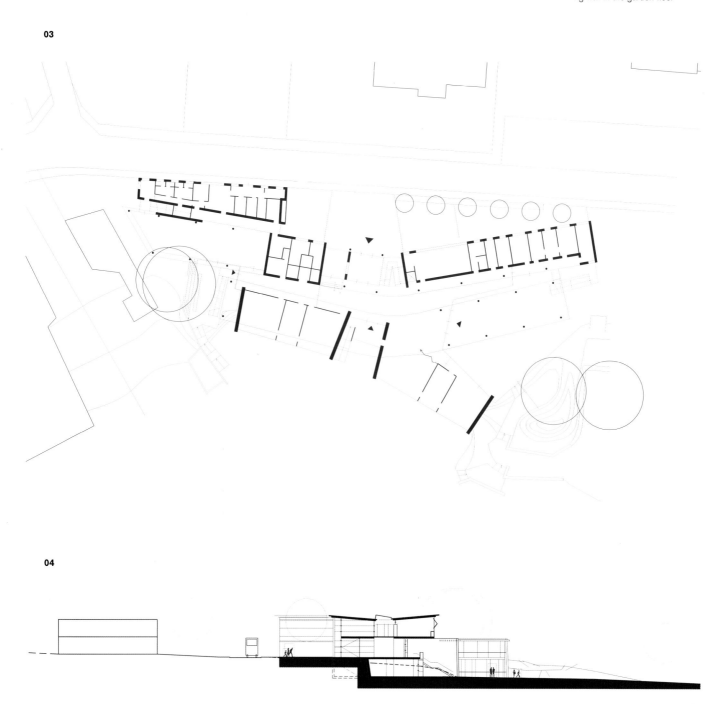

04

SolarCity Centre, Linz-Pichling, 2004
Address: Lunaplatz 1–4, 4030 Linz-Pichling, Austria.
Client: City Council of the Provincial Capital Linz /
Raiffeisen Immobilien-Leasing GmbH. **Gross floor
area:** 16,540 m².

Newtonian decomposition

ARCHITECTS: Auer+Weber+Assoziierte,
Stuttgart & Munich

The coloured glass surfaces in the SolarCity were inspired by Newton's decomposition of white sunlight into
the colour spectrum. The spectrum used here ranges
from light yellow to orange, from red and violet to light
blue. The colours rise and fall in intensity along the spectrum, reaches their peak at the centre of the scale, and
almost completely running out at each end. This allows
the designed glass panels to seamlessly blend into the
clear panels. Thanks to the use of colour in glass and
the accompanying clear technical style of architecture,
it was possible to dispense entirely with ornamental design; due to their colour alone the glass panels create a
kind of open-air "bazaar" that alters its mood continually
with daily and seasonal light changes.

03

04

05

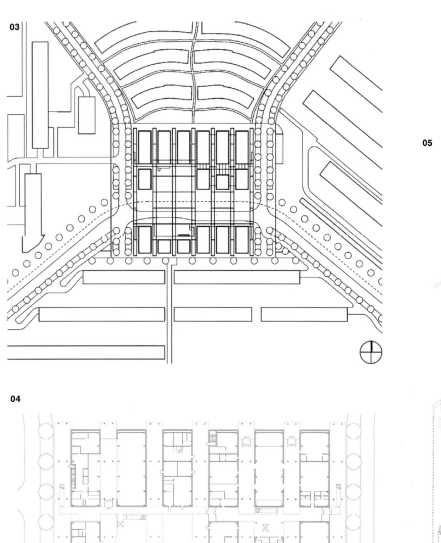

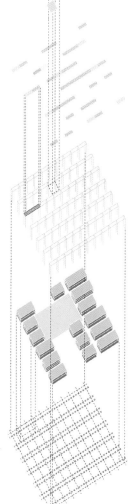

Refurbishment of the Frankfurt-Heddernheim urban rail station, 2005.
Address: Frankfurt-Heddernheim, Dillenburgerstraße, Germany. **Structural engineers:** Bollinger & Grohmann Ingenieure GmbH, Frankfurt am Main. **Gross area of platform roofing:** 632 m². **Materials:** granulated architectural concrete for windscreen walls and kiosk, post and railing façade as well as grill shutters for kiosk, steel structure and rib mesh cladding for platform roofing.

Inspired by Judd
ARCHITECTS: schoyerer architekten BDA

The architects' response to the complexity of the task undertaken here was to work in large dimensions, even though railway platform awnings do not normally call for a large-scale approach. But it is possible in this environment to make a strong and recognisable architectural statement by employing large, clearly contoured roof volumes, not unlike the approach of the American sculptor Donald Judd who places large cubes in a dialectic relationship to their surroundings. Unlike Judd's work, the cubes in this case do not rest on the ground but on pillars, thus forming signal roof elements. All concrete surfaces on the windscreen walls and the kiosk are deliberately coloured dark anthracite, thereby providing an excellent contrast to the colours on the metal surfaces. Just as the art of Donald Judd helped the roof cubes to anchor this place in a dynamic urban space, the architects also dipped liberally into Judd's colour pallet.

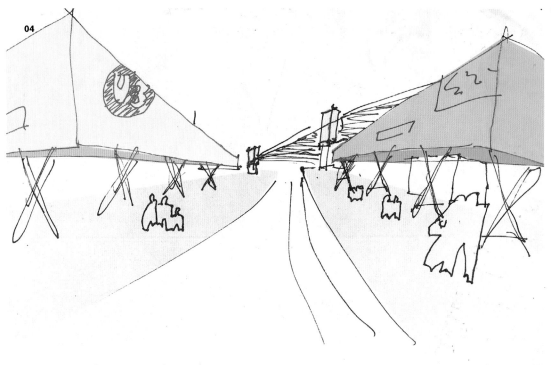

04

05

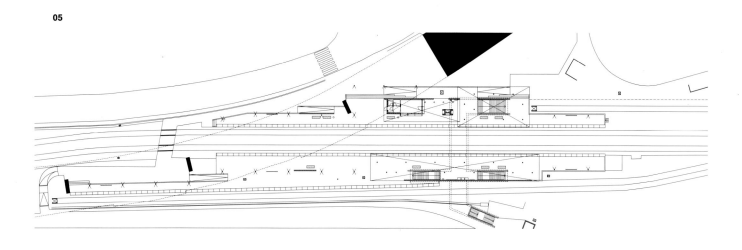

Celle Museum of Art with the Robert Simon Collection, 2006
Address: Schlossplatz 7, 29221 Celle, Germany. **Client:** Kunst-Stiftung Celle. **Gross floor area of new structure:** 1,100 m². **Materials:** reinforced concrete, steel, glass.

Just like the Empire State
ARCHITECTS:
ahrens grabenhorst architekten BDA

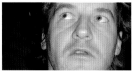

Celle is a North German town famous for its timber-framed houses and the architecture recalling its days as a residence of Saxon dukes. A new glass cube forms a radical extension to an old rendered building and a previous extension from the 1990s. The glass box makes no attempt whatsoever to ingratiate itself with or continue on from existing architectural elements. Rather, through a reduction in material and visual appearance, it creates a dynamic dialogue between the old and the new. Its message is surface, line and volume. Its surfaces are of uniformly reflecting clear and white matt glass – a precision achieved without glazing beads. The entire façade has been developed as a two-tier structure. At night the glass surfaces light up. Thanks to LED lighting strips it is possible to produce computer-controlled lighting animation in the full colour spectrum. On special occasions, for exhibition openings or street festivals the cube performs a show of various colour tones or lighting arrangements, just like New York's Empire State Building.

01 View from the Schlossplatz **02** Façade at dark **03** Ground floor **04** Longitudinal section **05** Façade at dark

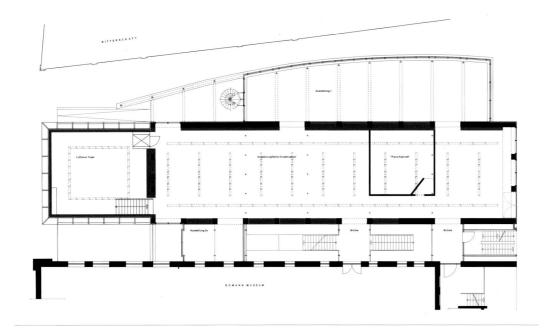

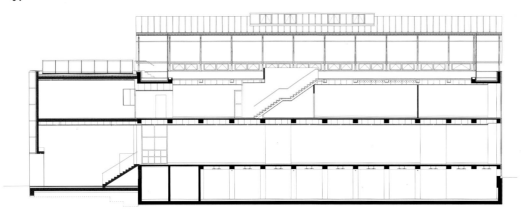

Public-access areas in the Spreepalais, 2004
Address: Anna-Louisa-Karsch-Str. 2, 10178 Berlin, Germany. **Client:** DEKA Immobilien Investment GmbH.

Palatial illumination

ARCHITECTS: Sergei Tchoban
nps tchoban voss GbR Architekten BDA
A. M. Prasch P. Sigl S. Tchoban E. Voss

The aim of this project was to enhance the public-access areas of the "Spreepalais" office building. The architect Sergei Tchoban developed an interior design concept that particularly focussed on this task. Important elements in his design include frosted and transparent glass plates with multiple lighting possibilities as well as warm wood panelling. These new design elements enter into a dialogue with the original design of the building, which contrasts natural stone and metal. Overall, around 100 illuminated sails – composed of glass plates and red/green/blue LED lights – were suspended in the winter garden, foyer and atrium areas. Using a special control mechanism, the colour and light intensity of the plates can be adjusted to daily and seasonal lighting conditions.

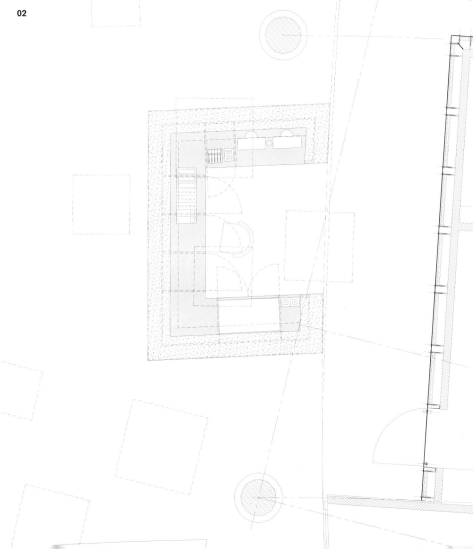

01 Foyer with bench elements **02** Counter plan **03 / 04** Glass plates with different lighting possibilities

236

**Lerchenfeld Freising Middle School
(Hauptschule), 2003**
A school with multi-use sports hall
Address: Moosstraße 46, 85356 Freising, Germany.
Client: Municipality of Freising, Mayor Dieter
Thalhammer. **Gross floor area:** 7,400 m². **Materials:**
concrete, steel, glass, wood, plaster.

Elegance in the sticks

ARCHITECTS: schulz & schulz, Leipzig

In this elegant school building colours and materials
are the guiding principles. An approach such as this always works well where the surroundings (as here) are
heterogeneous. The interplay between a bright colour
scheme and a clearly apparent sense of order makes
this school a friendly place that fits with a child's view of
the world. The deliberate contrast between colours and
wood, absence of colour and concrete increases this
effect. The break hall fronted by a flight of steps is the
main place where people meet, but can also serve as
a worthy location for events and assemblies. The corridor leading to the classrooms on the upper floors offers
space for children to play and relax. It also offers a com-
manding view of the entire school complex, right from
the classroom door.

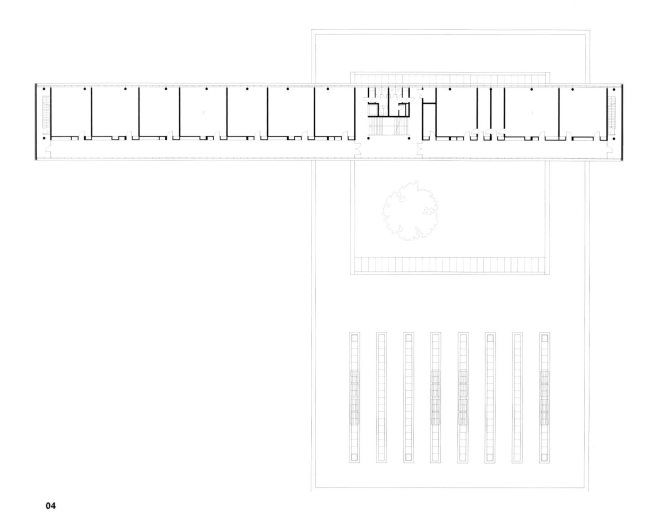

04

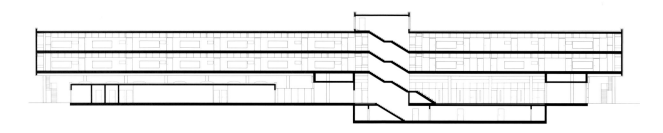

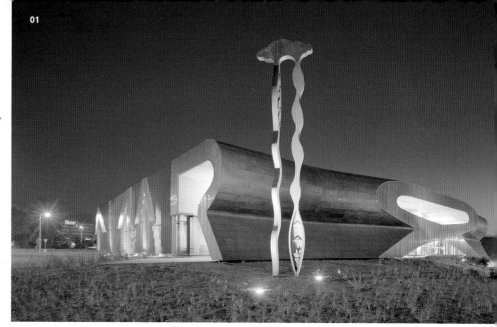

Marion Cultural Centre, 2002
Address: Milham St, Marion, Adelaide, Australia.
Client: Corporation of the City of Marion. **Materials:**
Walls: copper, precast concrete panels, timber battens,
steel; Roof: sheet metal roof decking (Fielders King
Klip 700). Paint: International Coatings (steel); Dulux
(concrete panels/internal).

The intensity of a thunderstorm
ARCHITECTS: ARM

The Cultural Centre complex at the "heart" of the city of
Marion near Adelaide houses a new library, café, community and tourist information centre, a multi-purpose
hall and meeting rooms. The development also includes
a plaza, art gallery and restaurant and there are plans
to incorporate an auditorium in the future. The project
places a strong emphasis on the inclusion of modern
technology. The energy-efficient design of the Marion
Cultural Centre incorporates a stormwater retention
system that allows surface run-off to be stored, filtered
on site, then pumped into the ground to replenish the
aquifer under Adelaide. The Centre also features a solar
hot water system, water efficient fixtures and fittings,
energy-efficient artificial lighting, low-energy evapora-
tive systems and economy cycle air conditioning. The
defining features of this building as announced formally
by the exterior, are mirrored within by the colour scheme
– intense as a thunderstorm, and fast as lightning.

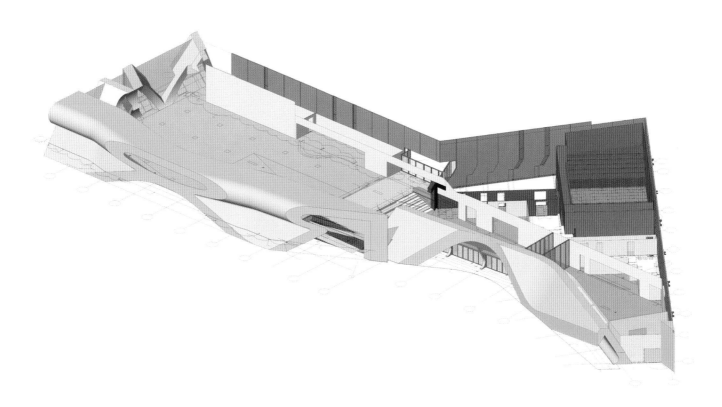

Selimex office building, Latsch, 2005
Address: Orteingang I, Latsch, Vinschgau, South Tyrol, Italy. **Structure:** Wolfgang Oberdörfer, Latsch. **Client:** Walter Rizzi, Selimex GmbH. **Gross floor area:** 2,393 m². **Materials:** steel structure, glass, trapezoidal sheet metal.

A miraculous feat of colour
ARCHITECTS: Werner Tscholl, Latsch

Those familiar with the architect Werner Tscholl appreciate his sensitive approach to the age-old South Tyrolean building tradition as well as its more flamboyant successors. Here he has created a latter-day fortified tower out of locally quarried stone, a modern work of light that with its cantilevered grid façade structure at the centre of a pool of water conveys a sense of the Far East. The bottle-green colour was chosen in reverence of the wine- and fruit-growing countryside that surrounds the building. The miracle takes place in the evenings when the genteel green dissolves in cascades of light thanks to 330 LED spotlights. The technology employed makes it possible for the cube to light up every day as the total energy consumption is less than three kilowatt hours.

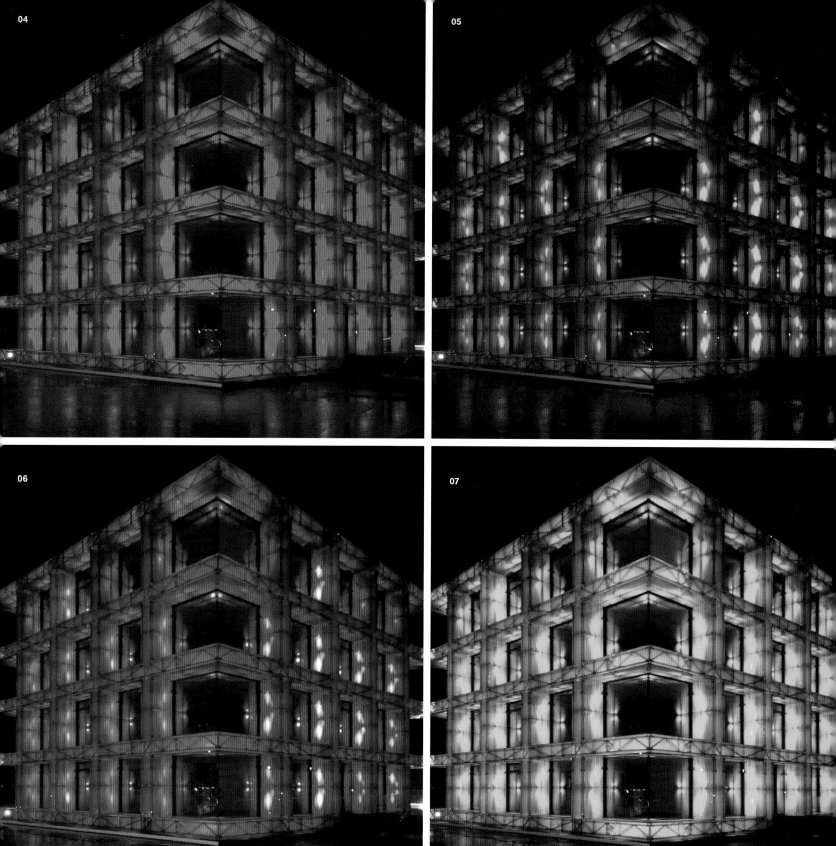

08

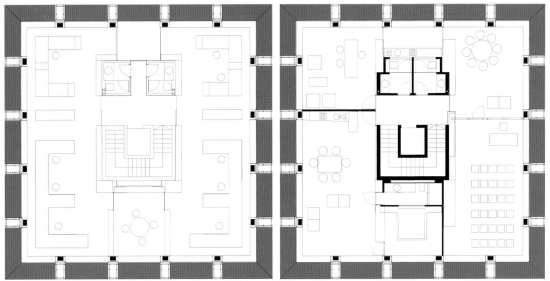

01 View by night **02** Cantilevered grid façade **03** Exterior view **04–07** Different lighting possibilities **08** Ground plans 1st and 3rd floor **09** Selimex site plan

09

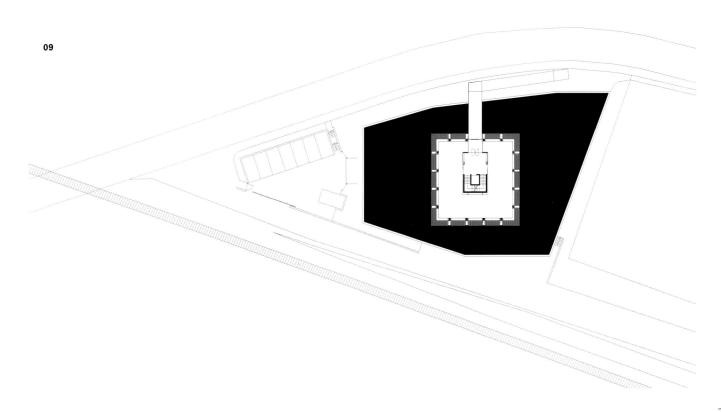

ARCHITECTS

INDEX

T +82.2.523.3443
F +82.2.523.5121
gaaarchitects@gmail.com
www.gaa-arch.com
→ 184

Gafner & Horisberger Architekten GmbH
Hardstraße 219
8005 Zurich (Switzerland)
T +41.44.350.42.26
F +41.44.350.42.27
arch@gafnerhorisberger.ch
www.gafnerhorisberger.ch
→ 156

gmp – Architekten von Gerkan,
Marg und Partner
Elbchaussee 139
22763 Hamburg (Germany)
T +49.40.88151.0
F +49.40.88151.177
hamburg-e@gmp-architekten.de
www.gmp-architekten.de
→ 112

GRAFT Lars Krückeberg,
Wolfram Putz, Thomas Willemeit
Kurfürstendamm 54
10707 Berlin (Germany)
T +49.30.24.04.79.85
F +49.30.24.04.79.87
berlin@graftlab.com
www.graftlab.com
→ 60

Gruber + Popp Architekten BDA
Am Spreebord 5
10589 Berlin (Germany)
T +49.30.68809665
F +49.30.68809666
office@gruberpopp.de
www.gruberpopp.de
→ 22

H

Bert Haller
Innenarchitekten
An der Eickesmühle 34
41238 Mönchengladbach (Germany)
T +49.2166.9463.0

F +49.2166.9463.22
www.bert-haller.de
→ 152

K

P. Karle / R. Buxbaum
Freie Architekten · Diplom Ingenieure
Bismarckstraße 15
64293 Darmstadt (Germany)
T +49.6151.28805
F +49.6151.28806
kabux@kabux.de
www.kabux.de
→ 104

KBNK architekten
Große Rainstraße 39a
22765 Hamburg (Germany)
T +49.40.399204.0
F +49.40.399204.22
office@kbnk.de
www.kbnk.de
→ 16

L

Lacoste + Stevenson
301/85 William Street
East Sydney NSW 2011 (Australia)
T +61.2.9360.8633
studio@lacoste-stevenson.com.au
www.lacoste-stevenson.com.au
→ 36

Henning Larsen Architects A/S
Vesterbrogade 76
1620 Copenhagen V (Denmark)
T +45.8233.3000
F +45.8233.3099
mail@henninglarsen.com
www.henninglarsen.com
→ 48

Lederer + Ragnarsdóttir + Oei
Kornbergstraße 36
70176 Stuttgart (Germany)
T +49.711.22.55.06.0
F +49.711.22. 55.06.22
mail@archlro.de
www.archlro.de
→ 136

LEGORRETA + LEGORRETA
Palacio de Versalles 285–A
Lomas de Reforma
11020 Mexico D.F. (Mexico)
T +52.55.5251.9698
F +52.55.5596.6162
info@lmasl.com.nx
www.legorretalegorreta.com
→ 38, 72

LEHEN drei Architekten Stadtplaner BDA SRL
Martin Feketics Leonhard Schenk
Matthias Schuster
Rosenbergstraße 52 a
70176 Stuttgart (Germany)
T +49.711.6409272
F +49.711.6076539
info@lehendrei.de
www.lehendrei.de
→ 66

M

Maedebach, Redeleit & Partner
Düsseldorfer Straße 38
10707 Berlin (Germany)
T +49.30.881.90.60.0
F +49.30.881.90.60.18
mail@maedebach-redeleit.de
www.maedebach-redeleit.de
→ 158

MANSILLA+TUÑÓN
Rios Rosas 11 6°
28033 Madrid (Spain)
T +34.91.3993067
circo@circo.e.telefonica.net
www.mansilla-tunon.com
→ 122

J. MAYER H.
Bleibtreustraße 54
10623 Berlin (Germany)
T +49.30.3150.6117
F +49.30.31506118
contact@jmayerh.de
www.jmayerh.de
→ 90

Schär Architekten AG
Höheweg 17
3006 Berne (Switzerland)
T +41.31.357.53.88
F +41.31.357.53.33
info@schaer-architekten.ch
www.schaer-architekten.ch
→ 208

schoyerer architekten BDA
Hauptstraße 17–19
55120 Mainz (Germany)
Postfach 240222
55045 Mainz (Germany)
T +49.6131.288481
F +49.6131.288488
architekten@schoyerer.de
www.schoyerer.de
→ 228

Roland Schulz, ars
Werderstraße 73
19055 Schwerin (Germany)
T +49.385.581.48.48
F +49.385.581.48.47
info@arslab.de
www.arslab.de
→ 26

schulz & schulz
Lampestraße 6
04107 Leipzig (Germany)
T +49.341.48713.3
F +49.341.48713.45
schulz@schulzarchitekten.de
www.schulz-und-schulz.com
→ 238

SEHW Berlin Hamburg Wien
Bogenallee 14
20144 Hamburg (Germany)
T +49.40.38.60.01.11
F +49.40.38.60.01.33
info.hamburg@sehw.de

Schumannstraße 21
10117 Berlin (Germany)
T +49.30.308785.10
F +49.30.308785.20

info.berlin@sehw.de
www.sehw.de
→ 14, 214

selgascano
José Selgas and Lucía Cano
Avenida Casaqumada 1
28023 Madrid (Spain)
T +34.9130.76481
F +34.9170.80315
selgas1@selgascano.com
www.selgascano.com
→ 42

she_architekten
Pilatuspool 7a
20355 Hamburg (Germany)
T +49.40.350.153.06
F +49.40.350.153.07
office@she-architekten.com
www.she-architekten.com
→ 20

Spengler · Wiescholek
Architekten Stadtplaner
Elbchaussee 28
22765 Hamburg (Germany)
T +49.40.389986.10
F +49.40.389986.33
office@spengler-wiescholek.de
www.spengler-wiescholek.de
→ 126

Steidle Architekten
Genter Straße 13
80805 Munich (Germany)
T +49.89.3609070
F +49.89.3617906
info@steidle-architekten.de
www.steidle-architekten.de
→ 162

T

Werner Tscholl
Morter-Mühlweg 11/A
39021 Latsch/Morter (BZ/Italy)
T +0049.473.742236
info@wernertscholl.com
www.wernertscholl.com
→ 246

U

Ben van Berkel / UNStudio
Stadhouderskade 113
1073 AX Amsterdam (The Netherlands)
T +31.20.570.20.40
F +31.20.570.20.41
info@unstudio.com
www.unstudio.com
→ 68, 200

V

Fermín Vázquez / b720 Arquitectos
Josep Tarradellas 123
08029 Barcelona (Spain)
T +34.93.363.7979
F +34.93.363.0139

Camino de Fuencarral 1D
28035 Madrid (Spain)
T +34.91.376.8214
F +34.91.376.8517
fermin.vazquez@b720.com
www.b720.com
→ 206

W

Wiechers Beck Architekten
Manteuffelstraße 77
10999 Berlin (Germany)
T +49.30.6162299.0
F +49.30.6162299.22
mail@wiechers-beck.de
www.wiechers-beck.de
→ 80

Clive Wilkinson Architects
144 N. Robertson Blvd.
West Hollywood, California 90048 (USA)
T +1.310.358.2200
F +1.310.358.2205
query@clivewilkinson.com
www.clivewilkinson.com
→ 76

Picture Credits

Ardiles–Arce, Jaime — 39, 41
ARS, Schwerin — 26, 27
Asin, Luis, Madrid — 122, 123, 125
Bennett, Valerie, London — 68 l., 128 l., 148 l., 200 l.
Bennetts, Peter, Melbourne — 242–244
Bettler, Lorenz, Zurich — 192 r., 193, 195
Bitter Bredt, Berlin — 128 r., 129, 131
Blaser, Christine, Berne — 208 b., 209
Bredt, Marcus, Berlin — 16, 17, 19
Bühler, Beat, Zurich — 156 b., 157
Buscher, Ralf, Hamburg — 126 a., 127
Camenzind Evolution, Zurich — 54 a.
Cappai, Carlo, Venice — 30 a.
Chan, Benny, Fotoworks, Los Angeles — 76–79
Chemollo, Alessandra, Venice — 31
de Maddalena, Gudrun Theresia, Tübingen — 66 b., 67
Dechau, Wilfried, Stuttgart — 112 l.
Douglas, Lyndon, London — 97
Ebeling, Frank, Cologne — 152 l.
Eicken, Thomas, Mühltal — 104–106
Firma Kleusberg, Halle — 135
Frahm, Klaus, Hamburg — 140, 141, 143
Franck, David, Ostfildern — 174–177
Gahl, Christian, Berlin — 86, 87, 89, 237
García, Óscar, Madrid (Grupo Agbar) — 206 a., 207
Gaultier, Alex — 168, 169, 171
Gebler, Christoph, Hamburg — 28 b., 29, 52 r., 53, 108, 109, 111
Görner, Reinhard, Berlin — 162, 163, 165
Graubner, Klaus, Frankfurt — 236 a.
Gregoric, Tomaz, Ljubljana — 172, 173
Günther, Ralf — 20, 21
Halbe, Roland, Stuttgart — 42, 43, 45, 136, 137, 139, 224, 225, 227, 232, 233, 235
Helbling, Bruno, Zurich — 192 l.
Heller, Steven, London — 96 l.
Hiepler Brunier, Berlin — 60 r., 61, 62
Hoffotografen, Berlin — 144 l.
Huthmacher, Werner, Berlin — 58 a., 59, 158, 159, 161, 220, 221, 223
Jeremy San of Stzernstudio — 182, 183
Johnson, Richard, Grand Rapids — 196–198
Joosten, Hanns, Berlin — 22–24
Kassner, Gerhard, Berlin — 228, 229, 231

Kim, Yong Kwan, Seoul — 184–186
Kisling, Annette, Berlin — 148 r., 149, 151
Kuns, Alexander, Berlin — 80 l.
Kuyas, Ferit, Wädenswil — 55, 57
Lacoste + Stevenson Architects — 36, 37
Latova, José — 38
Legorreta, Lourdes, Mexico D.F. — 72, 73, 75
Leiska, Heiner, Hamburg — 132, 133
Leistner, Dieter, Würzburg — 64 a., 65
Mørk, Adam — 48–50
Müller-Naumann, Stefan, Munich — 100–102, 210–213, 238, 239, 241
Nagaishi, Hidehiko, Tokyo — 188–190
Navarro, Jaime, Cali — 10, 11, 13
Pozo, Roberto — 32 l.
Richters, Christian, Münster — 68 r., 69, 71, 200 r., 201, 203
Ridecos, Ricky, Los Angeles — 60 l.
Ruault, Philippe, Nantes — 178, 179, 181
Ruchti, Jean–Jacques, Aarau — 54 b.
Ruspoli, Constantino, Milan — 30 l.
Scagliola, Daria, Brakkee, Stijn, Amsterdam — 216, 217, 219
Schmidt, Jürgen, Cologne — 14, 15, 214 a., 215
Scholz, Olaf — 28 a.
Siefke, Jan, Shanghai — 112 r., 113, 115
Soar, Timothy, London — 96 a., 99
Soenne, Aachen — 152 r., 153, 155
Sprenger, Lothar, Dresden — 116, 117, 119
Sumesgutner, Daniel, Hamburg — 144 r., 145, 146
Tiainen, Jussi, Helsinki — 166, 167
Tscholl, Werner, Latsch — 246–248
Verity, Allison, London — 96 b.
Walbeck, Nicola Roman, Düsseldorf — 94, 95
Wenborne, Guy, Santiago — 32 r., 33, 35
Wiechers Beck, Berlin — 80 b.
Wille, Tobias, Berlin — 80 a., 81, 83

All other pictures were made available by the architects

Cover
front side: Tomaz Gregoric, Ljubljana
back side: Christoph Gebler, Hamburg (l.)
Luis Asin, Madrid (r.)